D1206853

ALL ABOUT CARPETS
A CONSUMER GUIDE

GLENN REVERE

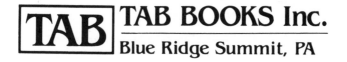

TAB BOOKS Inc.
Blue Ridge Summit, PA

ST. PHILIP'S COLLEGE LIBRARY

FIRST EDITION
SECOND PRINTING

Copyright © 1988 by TAB BOOKS Inc.
Printed in the United States of America

Reproduction or publication of the content in any manner, without express permission of the publisher, is prohibited. No liability is assumed with respect to the use of the information herein.

Library of Congress Cataloging in Publication Data

Revere, Glenn.
    All about carpets : a consumer guide / by Glenn Revere.
      p.   cm.
    Includes index.
    ISBN 0-8306-0646-7   ISBN 0-8306-0446-4 (pbk.)
    1. Carpets—Handbooks, manuals, etc. I. Title.
TS1775.5.R48   1988
698.9—dc19   88-20150
                                CIP

TAB BOOKS Inc. offers software for sale. For information and a catalog, please contact TAB Software Department, Blue Ridge Summit, PA 17294-0850.

Questions regarding the content of this book
should be addressed to:

    Reader Inquiry Branch
    TAB BOOKS Inc.
    Blue Ridge Summit, PA 17294-0214

Front cover photograph courtesy of Armstrong World Industries, Inc., P.O. Box 3001, Lancaster, PA.

Contents

Preface

Have you ever looked at the carpet under your feet and wondered from what it is made or how it is made? Or have you ever tried to buy carpet only to discover how bewildering it can be, with competing claims and fast sales pitches? Do you have questions about how the carpet in your home is installed? Or do you have a carpet that needs cleaning, but you've put it off because you don't know whom to call? This book answers these questions and many more.

I became a carpet inspector in 1973, after completing training in Philadelphia, and started a carpet inspection company, Professional Carpet Inspections, Inc., to handle claims for mills and retailers. (Training in carpet cleaning, repair, and installation is also part of the overall scope of my inspection business.) Over the years, countless individuals have asked me the same basic questions and have related to me the frustration they have had trying to find answers. People also become confused because they get conflicting answers from so-called experts. While salespeople, installers, and carpet cleaners all have valuable field experience, few of them are trained in all areas of carpeting. I decided that an easy-to-understand, but comprehensive, book was the best way to address the collective questions of consumers. A thorough guide would help to eliminate the confusion so many people have faced.

All About Carpets was written for the consumer. Carpeting is one of the largest investments most people make, after their home and car. All too often a consumer makes a decision to purchase carpet with very little information available on the subject. One can find out all about cars, appliances, and so forth; however, very little nontechnical material is available for consumers seeking practical advice about carpeting. The pamphlets published by the carpet industry are a good start, but they are sketchy and hard to find. This book is the first nontechnical carpet book widely available to the public. It is for people for want to make intelligent decisions regarding carpeting and the related areas of pads, installation, and maintenance. This book also answers your questions about carpet wear and performance, and helps you understand what to expect from your carpet. It explains basic interior decorating techniques and reveals effective ways to complain to dealers and carpet mills about defects or problems. The extensive glossary will familiarize you with terms used by people in the carpet industry.

The only area not extensively dealt with in this book concerns price as related to quality. As explained in the text, there are so many variables regarding carpeting prices that it is almost impossible to easily equate price and quality. A low price does not always mean a bargain; a high price does not always mean the best quality. Many other questions are answered, however, and knowing the right answers certainly helps you recognize a bargain. In this way, *All About Carpets* will help you save money.

I hope that making this book available to the public ends some of the confusion and makes people more aware of the expensive floor coverings in their homes. This book was written with the hope that it will help consumers make smart, satisfying decisions so that they are happy with their carpet and its performance.

Dedication

This book is dedicated to my parents for encouraging me
to start this book, and to my lovely wife, Eileen,
for encouraging me to finish this book.
I would not have finished it without her.
My deep appreciation to my publishers for their patience
throughout this entire project.

This book is also dedicated to the consumers
who will benefit from this book.

Acknowledgments

The author wishes to gratefully acknowledge the help of the following
people and companies:

L.D. Brinkman Company, Romane, Inc., That Floor Place, Highlands
Ranch Interiors, Adco Pro Chemical Supply and Sloane's Carpets
for the use of their showrooms; Adams Carpets for their help with
the installation sequence; and Mary Nielslinik for her photographic
technical assistance.

Introduction

A little history always puts things into perspective. The origin of rugs can be traced to the beginning of civilization itself. Scientists studying the Tigris-Euphrates area have found evidence of rugs dating to 2500 B.C. These rugs were probably woven of grasses and reeds or were made from animal skins. As the early civilizations learned to spin cotton and wool, the use of these fibers found their way into the weaving of rugs as well as clothes.

As civilization expanded, the use of rugs spread. The walls of Egyptian tombs more than 3000 years old show pictures of rugs, and the oldest rug in the Cairo museum dates to about 1800 B.C. Rug weaving developed into an art in countries such as Turkey, Iran, India, and China. When people discovered how to spin silk into thread, silk also became incorporated into rug weaving. The first oriental rugs came from these areas of the world.

The Greeks learned to use fine rugs when they conquered the Persians and Turks. The Romans derived their appreciation of rugs from the Greeks. In fact, *carpet* comes from the Latin verb meaning "to card wool." When the Turkish empire grew to include north Africa, Spain, and southern France, rug weaving spread to these areas.

But the art of rug weaving was perfected in China and India between A.D. 500 and A.D. 1200. The royal families made great use of fabulous rugs woven of gold, silk, and jewels. Marco Polo brought fantastic tales of beautiful rugs back to Venice after his travels to the Orient. About the same time, weaving appeared in Moslem controlled areas of Spain and was firmly established in the area by A.D. 1300.

Woven floor coverings are traced to England as early as the tenth century, but the few that were made were strictly for kings and their castles. These fabrics were more like mats than what we would call rugs. Most people continued to use straw mats over dirt or stone floors. With the royal blessing, the weaving trade began in England around 1350 and spread to France 100 years later when the first French guild for rug weavers was formed.

Another 100 years were to pass before Queen Elizabeth brought Persian weavers to England and firmly established the craft in Europe. England's damp climate created a demand for wool rugs, and what started as a fashion whim by royalty soon spread to the populace. By 1700, a sizeable rug-weaving industry was found around the town of Wilton, England. Other craftsmen quickly started a weaving center in the town of Axminster, England. By the middle of the eighteenth century, rugs were in widespread use throughout the cultured world.

Floor coverings came to this country with the first settlers. In fact, oriental rugs were prized possessions of the pilgrims, as were hand-woven rugs from Europe and England. Those who could not afford such luxuries used deer or bear pelts on the floors. Straw mats were also popular in colonial times. They were cheap and easy to make, and the natural fibers needed were found up and down the eastern seaboard. In the spirit of the "waste not, want not" ethic, rag rugs made from scraps of discarded clothing or other textiles were hooked and braided to grace the floors of many early homes. Some beautiful examples are found at the Smithsonian Institute's American History Museum in Washington, D.C.

But rug weaving, while one of the oldest ways to make carpet, is slow and tedious. In 1800, a good team of weavers could only make 6 to 8 yards of carpet in a 12-hour day. Therefore, rugs were only available to the rich. Around the same time in France, Joseph Jacquard invented a device for handlooms that predetermined the placement of colored yarns. By using a series of punch cards similar to a player piano, the Jacquard loom would produce the same pattern over and over. Changing the order of the cards or using different cards changed the pattern. This increased production. Also around the same time, Americans set up a carpet-weaving center in Philadelphia to make a 27-inch-wide fabric that was sewn into carpets of varying widths. The fine products gave Philadelphia an excellent reputation and made the area the center of American carpet manufacturing.

Around the middle of the century, Erastus Bigelow invented the first steam-powered loom and eventually combined it with the Jacquard mechanism. After inventing a power loom to make wider carpet, Bigelow began his own mill in Massachusetts. He further refined his inventions and licensed his machines to other manufacturers. The carpet industry gradually moved from Philadelphia to New England.

Carpet production increased markedly and price decreased to where factory-made carpeting was available to many more people. Production from one loom soon jumped to 75 yards a day! Gradual improvements made more types of weaves, and made them more quickly.

More improvements followed after the American Civil War. Power looms were modified to produce not only the Brussels weave (a modified loop pile) of the earlier power looms, but Axminsters, Wiltons, and others. The next 50 years brought increased popularity to carpet, but the basic manufacturing techniques did not change much until the introduction of tufted carpeting.

The idea of a tufted fabric originated during the 1920s with the quilters and bedspread makers living in the northern hill country around Dalton, Georgia. A widely used device was actually a modified sewing machine that stitched or tufted the designs and embroidery work into the bedspread. The early carpet tufting machines were modified bedspread tufters and were designed to make carpet 27 inches wide—the standard width for woven carpet.

As the demand for carpet rose dramatically after World War II, manufacturers began to look for faster, more economical ways to make carpet. The tufting machines were rapidly improved to make carpet in several widths, including 9-foot, 12-foot, 15-foot, and 18-foot widths. Tufted carpet became popular in the early 1950s, by offering quality at a price nearly everyone could afford. With a choice of several widths, an installer could fit a room with very few seams. Today, most carpet is available only in a standard 12-foot width. With modern tools and materials, an experienced installer can piece 12-foot goods together almost invisibly.

1
How Floor Coverings Are Made

Machine-woven carpet is very close in quality to handmade carpet. But now machine-powered looms are modified in many ways to produce effects such as intricate colorations and patterns not possible with handlooms. While only accounting for about 2 percent of the residential market, woven carpeting has attractive features, including strong construction and a wide range of colors and designs.

WOVEN CARPET

Axminster, Wilton, and *velvet* are the three major types of weaves found today. For all practical purposes, any of the three weaves will give excellent service and many years of enjoyment. The differences between Axminster, Wilton, and velvet are illustrated in Figs. 1-1, 1-2, and 1-3.

The back of all woven carpet is made by interweaving lengthwise and crosswise yarns to form the backing and face yarns simultaneously. Yet in order to grasp the workings and differences of the various types of weaves, you must first understand a few terms. (More terms can be found in the glossary.)

Heddle: A frame that holds warp yarns lengthwise, across which are drawn the weft yarns. The frame moves up and down to make an opening through which the

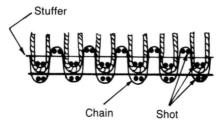

Fig. 1-1. The side view of an Axminster weave carpet.

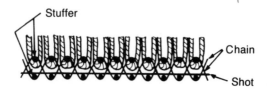

Fig. 1-2. The end view of a Wilton weave carpet.

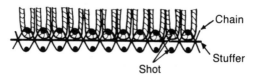

Fig. 1-3. The side view of a velvet weave carpet.

shuttle passes with the weft yarn. This mechanical action is the same as the over and under movement of a handloom.

Pick: Weft yarns that run between the warp yarns. The higher the number per inch, the tighter the weave.

Pitch: The number of lengthwise warp yarns in a 27-inch width of fabric. The higher the number, the finer the weave.

Shot: The number of widthwise weft yarns in relation to each row of pile yarns which help form the backing. Measured by the number of shots per inch, a higher number indicates a heavier carpet.

Shuttle: The long, narrow device that carries the weft yarns across the loom when the heddle opens.

Warp: Yarn that runs lengthwise down the loom.

Weft: Yarn that runs widthwise across the loom.

Wires: Also known as rows, wires are the number of tufts per inch that run lengthwise in a woven carpet. The more rows per inch, the heavier the fabric.

All weaving methods are similar. A loom is actually a frame with crossbars at each end. Lengthwise yarns are stretched between pins in the bars. These warp yarns run between slots in the heddle. The shuttle then passes through these slots with the weft yarns. As the frame moves up and down, it carries the warp yarns that bind with the weft yarns. Each time the heddle goes up or down, another row of fabric is formed. The *reed* is a comblike device that pushes each weft row against the preceding one to ensure a tight fabric.

To make carpet, a backing is formed along with the pile. The lengthwise part of the back is made by warp yarns called *chain* and *stuffer.* More than one chain can be used to bind the weft yarns to make a stiffer, heavier fabric. First, the chain (warp) yarns are threaded through wires fastened to the heddle and move with it. Second, the chain is wound on a cylinder above the loom and unwinds as the heddle moves. Next, the face warp yarns are fed into the loom separately by *yarn creels*—that is, yarn wound on special drums—in order to create the face pile. The face yarns are looped over wires that are perpendicular to the warp yarns. The thickness of the wire determines the pile height. Finally, the face warp yarns are woven into the backing yarns by shots of weft yarn. When the wires are removed, looped pile is formed. For cut pile, a knife is attached to the far end of the wire. When the wire is withdrawn, the knife cuts the loops.

Even by machine, weaving carpet is a tedious process. It takes a long time to set up the hundreds of creels that a loom requires, and once the loom is set up, the weaving process itself is relatively slow. Combine the slow manufacturing process with more costly yarns such as wool, and it adds up to a more expensive carpet. Fortunately, however, the quality usually compensates for the added expense. Woven carpets are usually heavy, thick fabrics that seem to wear forever. It would be difficult to select a poorly made woven carpet. They generally represent a high-quality investment and enhance any home.

TUFTED CARPET

A tufting machine is a giant sewing machine with as many as 1200 needles across the 12-foot width. Like a sewing machine, each

ST. PHILIP'S COLLEGE LIBRARY

3

needle stitches yarn supplied by a ball or creel into what becomes part of the finished carpet. A fabric known as the primary backing is fed by a roller system under the rows of needles. The needles puncture the backing and stitch the yarns into it. The yarn then enters from the back to the front of the primary backing and is tufted in lengthwise and upside down. The distance between the needles is the *gauge*, or tightness of rows of yarn, and is one indication of carpet quality. The closer the rows, the tighter and heavier the fabric (Figs. 1-4, 1-5).

Gauge is measured in rows per inch of width. For example, good quality kitchen carpet is often ⅒th gauge, meaning that there are 10 rows of tufts per inch across the width. Gauge is the same as pitch in woven carpet. Most common gauges are ⅛th and ⅒th, or 8 and 10 rows of yarn, respectively.

The diameter of the yarns being tufted will, to a certain extent, determine the closeness of the needles. A thick cable yarn cannot be tufted as closely together as a fine yarn simply because of its physical dimensions. Therefore, gauge is only one of several factors used to determine carpet quality. Generally, a good-quality carpet will have the rows tufted as closely together as possible.

Once the carpet yarn has been tufted into the primary backing, it is called the *face yarn*. The rows of face yarn usually run in straight lines. However, the rows can follow a zigzag or stepover stitch. The pattern is not important to the grade of carpet and primarily has to do with the type of equipment used.

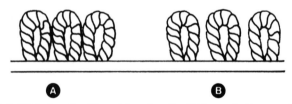

Fig. 1-4. High density (A) and low density (B) looped-pile carpet.

Fig. 1-5. High density (A) and low density (B) cut-pile carpet.

Most tufting machines are computer guided and can be easily programmed to produce varying results. The amount of needle penetration determines the length of the face yarns, commonly known as *pile height*. Normal tufting operations produce only looped pile, the same stitch used in garments (Figs. 1-6, 1-7, 1-8). Varying

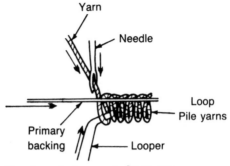

Fig. 1-6. Tufting looped-pile carpet. Stage one.

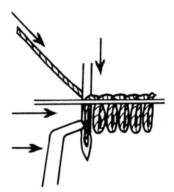

Fig. 1-7. Tufting looped-pile carpet. Stage two.

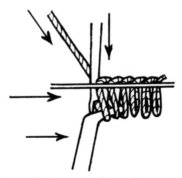

Fig. 1-8. Tufting looped-pile carpet. Stage three.

the pile height produces carved or scrolled patterns. To make cut-pile or plush fabrics, a knife is fitted to the tufting mechanism. As the loop of yarn is pushed through the primary backing, a knife hooks the loop and cuts it—forming two cut tufts from one loop. By tufting in two loops with one needle, four cut tufts can be stitched in for an even heavier fabric.

PRIMARY BACKINGS

The *primary backing* is the backbone of the finished carpet. The face yarns are tufted into the backing and form the pile. Primaries are both woven and nonwoven and are made from natural as well as man-made fibers. Woven primary backings are made from jute or polypropolene. Jute resembles fine burlap with round threads running in both directions. Polypropolene threads are flat and the finished fabric resembles a mesh. Nonwoven backings are always made from polypropolene. Fine threads or filaments are enmeshed to form a type of very thin yet very strong felt.

Proponents of jute backings like the way it readily absorbs the latex coating to create a well-bonded fabric. It keeps its elasticity in cold weather and stretches easily during installation. However, supply and price fluctuations due to trade conditions, international conflicts, and weather have forced many mills to use synthetic backings. Today, most of the world's supply of jute comes from Bangladesh.

Polypropolene is man-made from an oil derivative. Its generic name is olefin. In addition to a relatively stable supply of material, manufacturers also benefit from a fiber that is fairly inert. Jute will rot under wet conditions (like under a flower pot), while olefin is not affected by water. Therefore, outdoor carpet with olefin backings can withstand all types of weather. Carpets used indoors will resist flooding and water damage when made with olefin backings. Mildew cannot form on the synthetic fibers because the man-made material supplies no food for the mold that makes the mildew and rot.

Once the fibers dry out, the carpet returns to normal. If the face yarns are also synthetic, they too will resist water damage. The latex bond between the backings might be weakened by the water, however, depending on the latex's formula. If the bond is weakened, the primary and secondary backings will separate. This is known as *delamination*. Once delamination occurs, the carpet must be replaced because the fabric will wrinkle and become distorted.

Most backings are made in two shades, light or dark, depending on the color of the yarns to be tufted into the backing. Both jute and poly backs can be colored to match the color of the pile. When carpeting is installed over a step or a similarly curved place, the fabric can open along its rows to expose the backing. This is called "grinning." Even heavy fabrics will grin under the right conditions. A colored backing blends in better and creates the appearance of a thicker carpet.

Yarns tufted into the primary backing are only loosely inserted and must be strongly secured to remain locked into the primary and survive scuffing, pulling, and vacuuming. Once the face yarns are stitched in, the material moves under a roller that applies a thin, even coating of liquid latex rubber across the entire width. The latex acts as a glue and permanently binds the face yarns to the primary backing (Fig. 1-9). The amount of latex used is measured in ounces per square yard. Generally, the thicker the tufts and the tighter the gauge, the more latex is needed.

At this point in the manufacturing process, mills have an option. They can take various steps to finish the carpet, or they can add a secondary backing and then finish the carpet. Most carpet comes with a secondary backing that is used to cover the exposed latex rows (Fig. 1-10). It makes a stiffer, heavier fabric—one with more

Fig. 1-9. Latexed primary backing and face yarns.

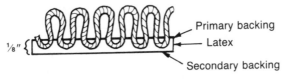

Primary backing
Latex
Secondary backing
1/8"

Fig. 1-10. Side view of tufted pile carpet. The secondary backing covers the rows of yarn.

"hand," or dimensional stability. This can be a help when installing the carpet.

If the designers have chosen to include a secondary backing in the product, it is applied to the latexed primary using rollers similar to those that fed the primary to the tufting needles earlier in the process. Once the secondary backing is on, the fabric passes through a heater that cures the latex. The yarns, latex, and backings are fused into a strong floor covering. The secondary backing is visible when the carpet is turned over.

SECONDARY BACKINGS

Secondary backings are made using the same materials as primary backings. Most are jute (Fig. 1-11) or olefin (Fig. 1-12) and

Fig. 1-11. Jute secondary back (tufted carpet).

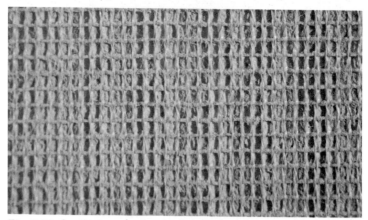

Fig. 1-12. Synthetic secondary back (tufted carpet).

are woven fabrics. A few nonwoven secondary backings can also be found. Because the secondary backing is basically a covering material, it is not necessary to weave it as tightly as a primary backing. Several grades of jute backings are used, with the closeness of the fabric determining the grade.

Woven olefin comes in a standard grade and is most commonly known by its trade name, Action-Bac olefin. Mills often switch between jute and synthetics, depending on price and supply considerations. Both materials give the same results. Secondary backings are left in their natural color because, unlike primary backings, they are never seen once the carpet is installed. The secondary backing also provides additional cushion for the face yarns, helping to prolong the life of the carpet.

The tufting machines combine the materials rapidly. Today's high-speed tufters make several hundred square yards of carpet in a day. Rapid production means lower prices. Because tufted carpet is made more quickly than woven carpet, it is less expensive than an Axminster or Wilton weave fabric. Also, woven carpets tend to use wool or wool-blend yarns, as befits the slower, more expensive manufacturing process. Tufted carpets tend to use synthetic yarns and benefit from their lower prices. The combination of large volume and lower-priced materials produces a less expensive carpet that still delivers a good value. In addition to lower price, tufted carpet is made in a wider variety of styles, patterns, and colors than woven carpets.

Another tufting technique produces needle-punched carpet. Here, face yarns are laid on the backing material and driven into the backing by barbed needles that enmesh the yarns in the backing. The fabric is latexed and a secondary backing is laminated to it. This system creates a low, dense face pile used mostly in commercial or outdoor applications.

Whether you choose woven or tufted carpet, the choice is so wide you are bound to find something to meet your needs—beautiful colors, long wear, and increased value for your home.

2

Distinguishing Yarn Types

When people shop for carpet, one of the first questions they ask about any style is, "What's it made of?" The selection of a proper face yarn, or pile, is the most important factor affecting the wear and performance of the carpet. Conflicting ads and claims are very confusing, as each one promises the ultimate carpet fiber. The different fibers all offer advantages and disadvantages to the consumer.

NATURAL FIBERS (WOOL)

Wool is the only natural fiber used today for pile yarns, and only a certain kind of wool is suitable for carpeting. Most sheep are raised in warm climates and grow soft fleece. This wool is ideal for clothing, but it is not resilient enough for floor coverings. The best wool for carpets comes from harsh climates in regions such as the Middle East, Scotland, northern China, and New Zealand.

Such a restricted supply cannot come close to meeting the world's demand for this luxurious resource. As a result, wool is a benchmark by which synthetic fibers are measured. It is the most expensive of all pile yarns and is used in higher-priced carpets. Yet even with its higher price, good-quality wool broadloom is economical because it lasts so long. It is common to see 20-year-old wool carpet still giving good service. In all, wool accounts for about three percent of total carpet production.

Advantages of Wool

Why does wool make such a good carpet? First, it is very soft yet very resilient. When walked on, it springs back to its original appearance. Under a microscope, wool filaments have a fish-scale look. This rough surface actually hides dirt, making the carpet look cleaner than it really is. The filaments also diffuse light that strikes the fabric, softening the color and general appearance. Wool wears well, but must be made in a denser fabric than some synthetics to hold up under heavy use.

Another reason wool makes excellent carpet is that it dyes easily. Because it readily absorbs water, it is very colorfast. Also, all wool carpeting made today is permanently mothproofed.

Disadvantages of Wool

On the negative side, because wool has a natural color and is not clear like the synthetics, it is more difficult to dye to a specified color. This means that there is more variation between a store sample and the actual roll of carpet that is installed. Also, wool stains more easily than most synthetics because it absorbs water and "draws" any color into its molecular structure. Fortunately, however, normal soil cleans out easily because the rough surface of the fiber releases dirt.

Wool produces static electricity under dry conditions, but a humidifier eliminates this problem. Furthermore, if allergies are a consideration, one might choose a fiber other than wool.

Processing of Wool

The story of going from animal hair to beautiful carpet for your home is a fascinating one. Each year great herds of sheep are shorn of their wool. The raw wool is then graded and further separated according to approximate color (light to dark). The wool is then shipped to a processor.

After blending several shades to obtain a fairly uniform color, the wool is cleaned. (Remember, sheep range wild and their fleece collects seeds and twigs. Also, sheep are branded with tar or pitch.) It is then untangled and carded.

Spinning the Wool

Natural lanolin in the wool helps lubricate the fiber. This marks the beginning of the spinning process. There are two systems, or methods, used to spin wool into yarn: the worsted and the woolen systems. (The same systems are adapted for spinning synthetic fibers.) Worsted systems produce woolen yarns in which only long fibers are used and are combed parallel, resulting in a harder, longer-wearing pile.

Woolen systems, on the other hand, create a yarn made up of wool fibers that are somewhat tangled and of different lengths. This type of yarn makes a softer pile that is bulkier but does not wear as well as worsted piles. Unfortunately, it is nearly impossible when buying carpet to tell if a wool pile is worsted or woolen. An honest salesperson can help here.

Dyeing the Wool

Once the fibers are spun into the desired yarns, the yarn is wound and prepared for dyeing. Two methods are generally used—skein dyeing and piece dyeing. Skein dyeing places many bundles, or skeins, in the dye vat at one time. It takes a lot of yarn to make one roll of carpet, and many rolls must be made from the same dye run, or dye lot. Large installations demand several rolls of carpet, and each roll must be virtually the same color so that when laid side by side there is no color variation. After dyeing, the skeins of yarn are wound on balls, or creels. The yarn is now ready to be tufted or woven into a floor covering to grace your home.

One can also tuft undyed yarn into a carpet and then dye the finished fabric. This is known as piece dyeing. The dye vats are so large that several rolls of carpet are placed in them at one time. The rolls are tumbled in the dye bath for several hours to ensure even coloring and a large dye lot.

SYNTHETIC FIBERS

Synthetic fibers are used in over 95 percent of all carpeting made in this country. A handful of giant chemical companies make the four types of carpet yarns: nylon, acrylic, polyester, and olefin. While these fibers are also used in clothing, the molecular structure of the filaments are different for carpet yarns because different characteristics are needed for long-wearing carpet.

Nylon

Nylon is the most popular carpet fiber. It accounts for up to 80 percent of carpet production. Nylon was developed in the late 1930s and was marketed most successfully in the 1950s and 1960s under the Du Pont trademark "501" nylon.

Advantages of Nylon. Nylon affords the carpet industry a steady supply of relatively low-priced yarn. But the early nylons had many other advantages over wool in addition to price. Nylon wears better using equal weights of face yarn. Also, it is easier to dye to a precise color because raw nylon has no color.

Nylon cleans as easily as wool but tends to dry more quickly because nylon fiber absorbs less moisture than wool (1 percent versus 17 percent for wool); and because nylon absorbs little water, stains do not set as easily as with wool. The foreign matter stays trapped between filaments until it is removed during cleaning.

Also, nylon has a "memory" that helps keep the face yarns twisted in the case of cut-pile fabrics. Built-in resiliency helps prevent crushing. This means that the carpet keeps its original appearance longer. In addition, nylon does not support mildew or mold, and is nonallergenic.

Disadvantages of Nylon. Nylon also has some disadvantages that have kept the chemists working overtime to eliminate. Static electricity is a big problem for both wool and nylon. Since nylon is man-made, it has been reengineered to avoid static buildup. This protection is built into the molecular structure of the filament itself and cannot be removed by cleaning or wear. This feature is found only in the third- and fourth-generation branded yarns. Neither generic nor early generation yarns offer static control.

An early problem with nylon was its coarse texture. Great effort has gone into making nylon with a soft "hand," or feel. This, too, is accomplished by manipulating the chemical structure of the nylon filaments. Some nylons are fine in texture and silky to the touch, but their wearability and cleanability are not diminished.

The first nylons were shiny. While manufacturers touted the luster of the carpet, consumers were used to softness and low luster from wool and resisted the "cheap" appearance of nylon. Much research and expense has created delustered nylon yarns with the same look and warm colors of wool.

This shine problem relates directly to poor soil-hiding properties. As stated earlier, wool's rough texture helps reflect light rays and hide soil. Nylon is like a clear plastic straw. Even if dyed, dirt shows through.

After years of experimentation, fiber manufacturers developed nylon filaments with light-scattering and soil-hiding properties. This is done by changing the round filament into one with a trilobular cross-

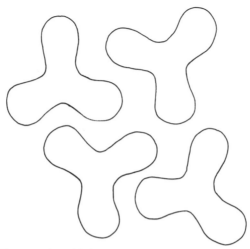

Fig. 2-1. Cross section of Anso brand nylon yarn made by Allied Signal Corp.

Fig. 2-2. Cross section of Antron brand advanced-generation yarn made by Du Pont Co.

section (Fig. 2-1), or a filament with four holes running parallel through it (Fig. 2-2). A hollow, squarish filament is made by a third manufacturer.

Production of Nylon

Nylon fiber is made from a petroleum derivative. Both solid chips and liquid formula are heated to boiling, and the solution is forced through a showerhead-like device with tiny holes, called a *spinnerette*. As the filaments are exposed to air, they harden into a continuous strand.

The shape and diameter of the filament is determined by the shape and diameter of the spinnerette holes. The filaments are then wound for further processing. Because the filaments are made in one long strand dozens of feet long, they are called *continuous filament* nylon.

BCF Nylon. Before being spun into yarn, the filaments are generally crimped, or bulked, by either a mechanical or chemical process. Bulked continuous filament nylon, or BCF, makes a denser, more resilient yarn. It also allows the mills the luxury of using a yarn which gives the appearance of more carpet than there really is.

Looped kitchen carpet (the most common kind) is usually made with continuous filament yarn (Fig. 2-3). That is why it runs in one long strand when snagged, like a nylon stocking. The filaments run in one continuous length through the carpet. When BCF is made into any type of cut-pile fabric, the carpet sheds very little, because all filaments are parallel and locked into the backing at the same place. Few are able to work loose from the latexed backing.

When the crimped continuous filament yarns are spun, they are twisted together to form a single-ply yarn. A *ply* refers to one strand. The thickness of the ply depends on the number of filaments twisted

Fig. 2-3. Tufted looped kitchen carpet.

together. The diameter of the ply affects the texture of the finished carpet. As a rule, carpet yarns are two or three ply. Once the filaments are twisted and plied, the yarn is wound and heat-set.

Heat-setting is a process similar to a permanent wave treatment—it gives the yarn a "memory." The finished yarn, through a variety of techniques, is put under heat, steam, and pressure for a predetermined length of time. When heat-set, the piled yarns stay twisted and resilient even with a lot of use and repeated cleanings. (Wool does not heat-set well and does not hold up when made into long napped carpets such as shag.)

Staple Yarn. Continuous filament fibers can be made into staple yarn instead of continuous filament yarns as described above. BCF is chopped into short filaments from 3 inches to 8 inches long. After a series of combing and blending operations, the staple fiber is ready for spinning into yarn. The process is the same for nylon staple as the process described earlier for spinning wool. Both the woolen and worsted systems are used.

Staple yarns are very popular with carpet mills and probably make up two-thirds of a typical mill's production. Although extra steps are needed to make the yarn, it has advantages over BCF. Staple yarns, regardless of fiber type, offer greater coverage than continuous filament yarns. This means that a given amount or weight of face yarn will appear heavier if staple rather than continuous filament yarn is used. To put this another way, more BCF yarn is needed to make a carpet that looks as thick as if it were made from staple yarn.

So why use BCF if staple looks heavier with less pile? Staple is by nature a fuzzier yarn than BCF. Because they shed throughout the life of the installation, staple fabrics cannot achieve the clean finish of continuous filament yarn. Staple is better suited to rougher textured fabrics. BCF's lack of shed or lint makes the carpet easier to maintain. The consumer gains because BCF is generally made into heavier carpets to look as nice as staple piles. Heavier translates into better wearing for about equal price—therefore a good value.

Because nylon fiber is very tough, it has excellent abrasion resistance. Just walking on a well-made nylon carpet will never wear it out, even with a lot of traffic. A carpet wears or gets thin because the yarn physically abrades away. This happens when the fabric is allowed to get dirty and remain soiled so that grit and sand actually cut away fiber. The cut fiber is vacuumed up, and the carpet slowly disappears.

Acrylic Fiber

Acrylic fiber was designed in the 1960s specifically as a man-made substitute for wool. The developers of this petroleum derivative aimed to duplicate all of wool's good points and improve some of its weak points. Its best known trade name is "Acrilan," made by Monsanto. Acrylic fiber is normally mixed with a modified form of acrylic called modacrylic, which is added to get better fireproofing from the finished yarn. However, "acrylic" is the general term for the mixture of both fibers.

Advantages of Acrylic. Acrylic dyes well. Like wool, it is stock or skein dyed. It is also solution dyed before extrusion into filaments. This makes a yarn which is very colorfast and does not sun fade easily. Solution-dyed acrylics are used in some outdoor carpeting and work especially well around pools and on boats where other fabrics would not hold up.

The chemists generally succeeded in reaching their goals. Acrylic looks and feels like wool. It is available only in staple forms and is spun like wool. It is soft and very bulky and is distinguished from wool only by a slight luster.

Acrylic is static-free and nonallergenic. It is also fairly stain resistant, although it is harder to clean overall soil from acrylics than from wool or nylon. Acrylics are generally made in heavier fabrics in order to resist crushing.

Disadvantages of Acrylic. While abrasion resistance of acrylic is high, its crush resistance is low. This should be expected from a high bulk, soft yarn. Acrylics are most often found in heavy plushes or two- or three-ply looped fabrics. Like all staple yarns, acrylic pile always sheds somewhat. The amount is determined by the length of the staple fiber. The longer the staple, the less fuzzing and shedding will occur. However, the consumer must trust luck in this area because staple length information is usually not available to salespeople.

A better-quality carpet should use a long staple fiber, but there is no guarantee of this because no industry-wide standards exist.

Acrylic yarns account for about 5 percent of total sales.

Polyester Fiber

Polyester, another oil derivative, was developed around the same time as acrylic. Available only in staple form, polyesters first attracted attention because of its crisp, clear colors. Many mills made polyester carpeting in every color of the rainbow, and consumers responded by creating quite a demand for the new fiber.

Unfortunately, polyester yarns were often made in single-ply. These "singles" yarns had no resiliency, and the carpets matted badly and simply flattened out in high-traffic areas. Needless to say, many consumers felt cheated and polyester got a very poor reputation. This is probably a reason why nylon quickly gained consumer acceptance and its use rocketed. When polyester was made only in two-ply yarns, it began to slowly win back some of its markets. Today it accounts for less than 5 percent of all carpet yarns.

Advantages of Polyester. Polyester has its good points. It dyes well and is made in beautiful colors. It is a very tough fiber and resists abrasion or wear, especially in heavier fabrics. Since it costs less to make, it falls into the more popular price ranges.

Also, the filament has a soil-hiding cross section. It is low in static and is nonallergenic. Like the other synthetics, it will not support mildew. It can be solution dyed before extrusion into filaments, making it very colorfast and fade resistant.

Furthermore, polyester is hydrophobic. This means it absorbs almost no water. This characteristic results in a fiber that is difficult to stain because the stain is not absorbed into the filaments. Instead, the foreign matter stays between the filaments, making it easier to remove the stain.

Disadvantages of Polyester. Polyester also has some disadvantages. Because it is a staple fiber, it can fuzz or "pill." This happens when fibers slip from the backing and ball up like an old sweater. Polyester, like acrylic, is a soft fiber. Its resilience is lower than wool or nylon and it has a tendency to crush down in high use areas, even using the two-ply yarns.

While it is fairly easy to spot clean, polyester is one of the more difficult yarns to clean overall. Even though all published information indicates it cleans well, carpet cleaners know better, because in actuality polyester does not clean easily, no matter which method is used. It is recommended that polyesters be cleaned more frequently than nylon or wool to prevent a buildup of soil which otherwise cannot be completely removed. Trevira-brand polyester seems to clean best.

Olefin Fiber

Polypropolene, or olefin, is another type of fiber used in carpeting. It, too, is made from an oil base and is extruded into filaments. It is the newest of the synthetic fibers, probably accounting for less than 5 percent of all carpet pile yarns.

Advantages of Olefin. Olefin has many advantages. It is used in both primary and secondary backings. When used as pile yarns, it is strong and resists abrasive wear. It is only solution-dyed, and is very colorfast and fade resistant. When a special chemical is added to the dyestuff before extrusion, the yarns will not sunfade.

Also, olefin is a bulky yarn that provides good cover when used in continuous filament or staple form; a relatively small amount of face yarn can look like a heavy carpet. It is practically static-free, will not mildew and is nonallergenic.

Furthermore, olefin cleans extremely easily. Like polyester, it is hydrophobic and will not stain. Today, it is mostly used for commercial applications as a level-loop fabric, although some residential and cut-pile fabrics are available.

Disadvantages of Olefin. Olefin's main drawback is that it is not very resilient and tends to crush and look worn out in high-traffic areas. This is the reason why olefins are most often found in looped-pile carpets. The looped fabrics are more resistant to crushing than cut-piles.

In addition, the colors tend to be somewhat muddy instead of clear and crisp like polyester, and the color range is generally limited. This is because of olefin's water resistance. If water cannot penetrate the fiber, dyes are difficult to apply. That is why most olefins are solution dyed. The fibers can also be chemically modified to accept dye after extrusion into filaments, but the range of colors is small.

Olefin has a low melting point. Friction from the wheels of a child's toy race car can melt the face yarns. Under most circumstances this is not a problem, however.

All of today's yarns are made into vibrant, beautiful carpets. Knowing the benefits of each type will help you make your final selection.

3

Carpet Styles and Textures

Any of the carpet fibers mentioned in Chapter 2 can be made into a wide variety of textures and patterns. Each connotes a certain style, ranging from casual to formal elegance.

Texture is made in many ways. Tufted carpet has a flat level-loop when produced in the normal manner. By changing the tension of the yarn, high and low loops are attained. By cutting the loop, it becomes a cut-pile.

Combining cut and uncut pile produces different textures. By extending various combinations, entire families of new textures materialize. Adding colorations further changes the apparent textures. One or another of these variations is always in style. Improvements in weaving techniques have also produced carpet with many more textures.

With so many different texture combinations, it is necessary to divide them into two primary groups: *loop-pile* and *cut-pile* fabrics. The loop-piles include level-loop, high-low and patterned loop, and tip-shear. The cut-pile group includes cut-pile (plush or velvet), cut and loop, multilevel and patterned, shag and mini-shag, saxony, and frieze (pronounced free-zay').

LOOP-PILE

Level-loop describes the weaving or tufting of face yarns into a carpet which appears flat and is made of rows of looped face yarns all the same height (Fig. 3-1). It is the best wearing of all textures because more face yarns are exposed to the surface and is used in kitchen-type carpets as well as in commercial installations (Figs. 3-2, 3-3). The shorter the pile and the closer the rows, the better wearing the carpet.

Fig. 3-1. Level-loop carpet pile.

Fig. 3-2. Kitchen carpet.

Fig. 3-3. Commercial carpet.

Fig. 3-4. Wool berber tufted carpet.

Fig. 3-5. High-low loop carpet.

The term *round wire* refers to level loops which are drawn over a round wire during the weaving process. From the surface, both woven and tufted fabrics appear the same and, if made with the same fibers and face weights, both should wear the same. The very popular wool berbers are also level-loop fabrics (Fig. 3-4).

High-low loop carpets are made by both tufting and weaving (Fig. 3-5). The texture is created by making some loops high and some loops low. If alternating rows are high and low, a corrugated appearance is effected (Fig. 3-6). If the high and low loops appear randomly, the effect is a rough, casual appearance.

This texture, like level-loops, wears extremely well, allowing for variations due to yarn type. It has a tendency to crush slightly more than level-loops because of the longer loops. The longer the fabric, the more it will crush, whether it is looped or not. High-low loop is a good style for high-traffic areas such as family or rec rooms, kitchen, offices, or stores, wherever a casual look is needed.

Scrolled or *carved* carpet is a patterned high-low loop variation (Fig. 3-7). This is a classic style always popular with homeowners. A pattern, usually a leaf or its variation, is made by high and low loops and appears carved into the face of the pile. The depth of the pattern depends on the thickness of the material. The design originated with hand-carved Oriental rugs. A carved pattern is used with a formal setting and wears well.

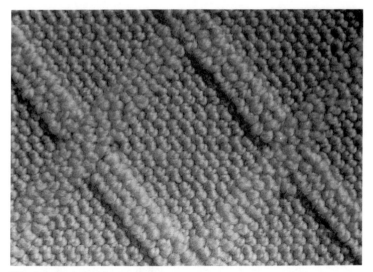

Fig. 3-6. High-low loop carpet.

Fig. 3-7. Carved carpet pile.

Fig. 3-8. Tip-sheared carpet pile.

Tip-sheared fabrics are found in both residential and commercial applications (Fig. 3-8). It is made by cutting and shearing some loops while leaving others looped. Tip-shearing can create different patterns such as a varigated loop alternating with rows of cut and

Fig. 3-9. Tip-sheared carpet.

uncut pile (Fig. 3-9), or random shearing which gives a dappled effect. Tip-shearing combines the best of plush and looped-piles. The evenness of the plush is broken up by the rugged texture of the loops. Tip-shear combines a casual and formal look. The cut portions are smooth and elegant, while the loops hide footprints and shading.

CUT-PILE

Cut-pile is the second main texture group. It refers to any style fabric that is made from cut instead of looped face yarns. Velvet plush (Fig. 3-10) and saxony plush (Fig. 3-11) are both smooth, heavy, velvety piles of cut-face yarns that are all the same height. Velvet plush is made of singles (unplied) yarn tufted or woven so tightly that the yarns support each other and stand up. The yarn ends seem to blend together when sheared smooth. This texture is the most formal of all and is very popular. (Velvet also refers to a particular method for weaving cut-pile fabrics.)

A *saxony* looks very similar to a velvet plush with its low profile and smooth finish. But instead of singles yarns, it is constructed of tightly plied yarns. The result is an elegant appearance that can stand up to high traffic. It is popular in residential, as well as commercial, applications. Like a plush, it shows footprints and vacuum marks. It can crush in high-traffic areas and show traffic patterns.

Fig. 3-10. Velvet plush pile.

Fig. 3-11. Saxony plush pile.

Plush fabrics must be made in relatively heavy weights (compared to loop piles) to wear well and maintain their original appearance. They also show footprints and vacuum marks and generally need more maintenance than loop fabrics.

Cut-and-loop fabrics are generally casual designs, with some yarns cut and others looped (Fig. 3-12). The pattern can be one height only, or it can be high and low creating a cobblestone effect (Fig. 3-13), flowers, or swirls (Fig. 3-14). The pattern is also varied by using shag instead of plush in the cut-pile portion of the design. Cut-and-loop probably provides the widest design variations of all the styles. When the loops are multi level in height, more patterns are created, or the overall effect can be random. This style hides dirt and stains since it usually comes in multicolor tones. It is easy

Fig. 3-12. Cut-and-loop pile.

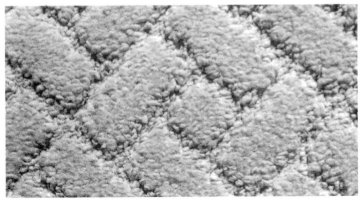

Fig. 3-13. Cut-and-loop pile.

Fig. 3-14. Cut-and-loop pile.

Fig. 3-15. Shag carpet.

Fig. 3-16. Shag carpet.

to maintain because it does not show footprints or traffic patterns as much as plush.

Shag is the longest cut-pile style (Fig. 3-15). Its popularity began in California where it was equated with an easy-going, open lifestyle. It started as a 2-inch-long, floppy fabric and soon evolved into shorter,

26

Fig. 3-17. Frieze pile.

Fig. 3-18. Frieze pile.

denser styles which were easier to vacuum. The government defines shag as any pile longer than ¾ inch, but shag is generally longer than 1 inch (Fig. 3-16). Cut-and-loop textures are also made in shag carpet. Most people call them long saxonies today.

Frieze is another classic style (Fig. 3-17). It appears to be a textured plush, but it is actually made of plied yarns that are tightly twisted and heat-set. It is tufted or woven into a cut-pile which is low, dense, and characterized by the twisted, kinky nature of the face yarns (Fig. 3-18). Friezes are known for their excellent wearability. They lend an informal air to any room, and hide traffic patterns and footprints.

CARPET AND INTERIOR DESIGN

Now let's review the different styles and textures according to room use. The living room is usually the showcase of the home. It is the first room guests see upon entering your home, so it must look attractive and comfortable. If your living room is more for looking than living—if it is not used much—then you can make use of light colors and delicate fabrics. Consider plush or saxony, perhaps even a wool berber in a pastel shade. If the living room has the TV in it, then it gets a lot of use. Somewhat darker colors or a subtle pattern might be just the thing. A tip-shear might work well, or try a patterned loop that avoids "walking out". A rougher texture will take the spills and a heavier fabric will hold up under the use a busy room receives.

The dining room is often attached to the living room, so it becomes an extension of the living room. Whatever you use in the living room will work fine in the dining room. If the room is off by itself, you might consider a fine plush, especially if the active living room has a carpet with a more casual texture.

The halls and steps of any home are the main traffic areas. It makes sense to put the sturdiest carpet and pad in these areas. The investment is well worth it. A heavy frieze, very tightly twisted low profile cut-pile, or even a level-loop will hold up under a lot of traffic. And remember, when a carpet is folded over the edge of a stair tread, the fabric has a tendency to separate along the rows of yarn and show the backing. Grinning can be avoided by using a heavy carpet.

The bedrooms are good areas to economize. They normally receive little usage because they are empty most of the day. Putting a heavy pad under a lighter weight carpet is an easy way to give luxury feel to a less expensive carpet. A better pad also makes the carpet wear better.

Lighter colors work well in a master bedroom, making the room look larger and more relaxing. Any texture works well, depending on your taste and decor. Try plush or saxony, or maybe a cut-and-loop for variety. Subtle patterns or colorful pastels work well in a girl's room, and make your child feel good about herself. A boy's room usually needs darker colors or prints. A sturdier fabric, like nylon, gives excellent service. Consider cut-and-loop or tip-sheared styles.

Many people like to carpet their kitchen. Of course, darker colors or patterned textures hide soil and spills. But if the family is neat, try lighter colors or pastels in a level-loop or frieze. A short pile makes it a lot easier to take care of the carpet. For a more formal look, consider a short saxony in one of the advanced-generation nylons. Whatever you choose, plan to clean it regularly so it always keeps its appearance.

What about the bathroom? Most new homes come with carpeted baths as an extension of the nearest bedroom. Some people feel that wall-to-wall carpet in a bathroom is unsanitary and difficult to clean thoroughly. For them the answer is washable area rugs or bath carpet. Whatever you choose must be sturdy because the floor covering gets a lot of confined use, as well as high humidity and direct water. If you decide to put wall-to-wall carpeting in a bathroom, make sure any cut-pile used has a tight twist. A low pile helps prevent crushing in front of the sinks and vanities.

4

Colors that Dazzle

Color is the most important consideration when buying carpet. The color not only beautifies the home, it ties together the rest of the furnishings. The carpet mills put a lot of time and effort into their color lines so that consumers will have a huge array of colors to choose from. The right colors in a new line can make it instantly popular.

CREATING NEW COLORS AND STYLES

The creation of new patterns and colors is a slow and tedious process. Generally, the larger mills have in-house artists who are attuned to the latest trends and styles. They often work closely with other fabric designers in the home furnishing industry, such as upholstery and drapery designers, to speculate on color trends 2 or 3 years from now.

The artists work with graph paper, literally plotting out each tuft of each new pattern. Different color combinations are created and committees cull what they hope will be popular colorations and textures. Then the machines are set to produce trial runs in order to see if the finished product looks as good as the artist's rendition.

Just because something looks good on paper does not mean that the fabric is something that a shopper will want to buy. In fact, many "mill trials" never make it to the carpet shops.

Design and style are two factors which help determine the final price of a carpet line. High fashion and a wide choice of colors are found only in the higher-priced lines. Whatever is "hot" will cost more. Smaller mills usually do not employ their own textile artists, and sometimes resort to copying popular designs from other mills in order to stay competitive.

DYE METHODS

Approximately 20 different dye methods are used today by the carpet industry. Each gives the carpet a different look. Seven techniques are used to dye most carpet. Included are piece dyeing, skein dyeing, space dyeing, print dyeing, as well as stock, solution, and TAK dyeing.

Piece Dyeing involves taking the freshly tufted carpet and placing it into a dye tank, or *beck*. Most dye becks can handle up to 400 running yards of *greige goods*, or undyed carpet. The dyeing process is performed before the secondary backing is put on. The carpet in the tank is stirred by rollers for several hours while pumps circulate the dye evenly.

Piece dyeing is used for wool and all synthetics except polyester and olefin. It creates a solid color fabric. This method is a simpler and less expensive dye system than most and is widely used in the industry for tufted carpet.

With *skein dyeing*, carpet yarn in the form of a skein is dyed by dipping the skeins in a hot liquid dye bath. The dyestuffs are circulated through the skeins, ensuring even color, while the dyes are heat-set. The dyed yarns are ready for tufting or weaving as soon as they are dry. Nylon and wool are commonly dyed using this method.

Space dyeing uses two different systems to produce an interesting effect whereby yarns are alternately dyed with three or more colors. One way lays hundreds of strands of yarn parallel to each other. A series of rollers print a different color on each section of yarn. After fixing the color, the yarns are washed, dried, and wound in preparation for tufting.

With the second method, sheets of knitted yarn are printed by rollers. Each roller puts one color on each side of the fabric. When finished, the colors are set and the yarns are washed and dried after unraveling. They are ready for tufting or weaving into a random tweed pile. Nylon is the most common fiber dyed by either of the two methods.

Print dyeing is a widely used technique that imitates the colors and patterns of woven carpets. This method uses equipment similar to a printing press. The pattern may be flat-printed or rotary-printed in multiple colors directly onto the tufted carpet.

Flat or *screen printing* is an offshoot of silk screen painting. Screens or templates outline the pattern. Dye is forced through the screen, transferring the pattern to the carpet pile. The dye does not necessarily penetrate the secondary backing.

Each color requires a different screen to produce a different section of the pattern. The Zimmer flat-bed print machine is one of the most popular systems. This machine uses a magnetic squeegee pressure system to apply the dye across the screens.

In *rotary printing*, the carpet passes against cylinders that have a raised, embossed pattern coated with dye. As the carpet passes against each roller, the design is transferred to the carpet. Each cylinder uses one color so that passing a carpet under several cylinders in a row makes a multicolored pattern.

In *stock-dyeing*, staple carpet fibers are dyed in bulk before being spun into yarn. Heated dyes circulate through large batches of fiber of up to 1000 pounds in each pressurized dye vat. Several batches of fiber dyed this way are then blended to ensure even color throughout the entire lot.

A steam chamber is used to set the dye. The fibers are washed, dried, and blended again. Then they are ready for spinning into yarn. Wool and nylon are commonly dyed this way.

Solution dyeing involves only man-made fibers, including nylon, acrylic, polyester, and olefin. Olefin is the most common solution-dyed fiber. Dye, either in chips or in liquid form, is mixed with the raw chemicals used to produce the still liquid fiber. When the mixture is drawn through the spinnerettes and formed into fiber, the dye color becomes part of the molecular structure of the yarn and the yarn is both colorfast and fade resistant. It is used in tufted carpets and is suitable for outdoor use and around swimming pools.

TAK dyeing is used on nylon fabrics. The carpet is given a base color and is then passed under a device which dribbles controlled amounts of a darker or contrasting color onto the pile. This system gives the carpet a "frosted" look, with a random pattern. A variation called gum-TAK dyeing makes a carpet with a dark base, white pile tips, and a mixing of colors in between the light and dark tones.

COLOR CONSIDERATIONS

Of course, all of this just explains *how* the carpet is colored. The most important thing to most people is the color itself. What color will look best in one particular room or throughout your home? How should you choose the right color that will make the right statement?

You've probably seen all the latest colors in the home magazines and fashion publications, and you've tried to keep up with the latest color trends. But what about your own color preferences? After all, we're talking about *your* home, not some abstract picture in a magazine.

It is important to start with a certain color in mind, but remember to be flexible. Designers are always coming up with new colors, tints, and shades, and you just may walk into a carpet shop and fall in love with a color you didn't even know existed. When looking for a color, take a paint or upholstery sample along. A color might look wonderful under the showroom lights, but might look dull or unattractive in your own home with different colored lights and walls.

But before you can choose a color, you must first understand a few basic things about how colors are made. *Primary colors*—red, yellow and blue—are colors already broken down into their basic components. Combinations of these three colors will make an almost infinite number of other colors and shades. A *color family* is formed by mixing the primary colors. There is a red/yellow family, a yellow/blue family, and a blue/red family. (Red and yellow make orange, yellow and blue make green, and blue and red make purple.)

Black and white are not technically considered colors. Black is a mixture of all colors, and white is the absence of any color. Tints are made by adding white, and shades are made by adding black. Black tones down bright colors without detracting from them. White does the same thing and works well to moderate lighter colors.

Color Schemes

Once you have chosen a particular color, you are ready to devise a color scheme. All color schemes are variations of the three basic ways to combine colors described above. Remember: choosing a color scheme is just a matter of taste. There is no absolute right or wrong way to do it.

The three basic types of color schemes used to integrate the colors in a room and pull the room together are monochromatic, analogous, and complementary.

One color, or *monochromatic*, color schemes use one basic color along with tints (light) and shades (dark) of the same color. Blue can be used as a basic color, with violet and plum as accents.

Two or more related colors make an *analogous* color scheme. For example, smoky brown and eggshell work well together. Or plum, violet, and rose are a lovely combination. Plum could be used as the overall color, with violet and rose as the accents.

A *complementary* color scheme uses contrasting colors to create a dramatic setting. One color serves as the dominant scheme, the other color becomes the accent. Plum with pale yellow is a good example.

Designing Tips

Keep these ideas in mind when considering color combinations:

○ Whenever possible, use the carpet and walls as the basis for your color scheme. They are the largest areas in a room, and you should plan around them for a unified design.

○ When using darker shades for the carpet, the walls can be a lighter shade of the carpet.

○ When using a light carpet, darker walls work well.

○ Light carpeting makes a small room look larger. Darker colors make a large room look smaller and more cozy.

○ Draperies work well to coordinate a color scheme when their color relates to the carpet, either through the pattern or by working with solid colors.

○ Bright warm colors work well in dark, poorly lit rooms and make them more appealing and cheerful. Sunny rooms will look cooler by using darker, more subtle colors.

○ A well-conceived color scheme sets the mood of a room. Bright colors are more informal; elegant, subtle colors make a room more formal and conservative.

Your designer will be happy to work with you to design the home of your dreams!

5

Carpet Padding

Padding is an underlay that goes between the carpet and floor. The proper padding is extremely important because it acts as a cushion to prevent the carpet, when walked upon, from bottoming out and rubbing the hard floor beneath. Such friction helps wear out a carpet.

Even though proper padding is so important, it is often only an afterthought that consumers have when purchasing a carpet. Remember that by putting a little extra into a better pad, you can extend—sometimes double—the life of your carpet. In addition, most pads are guaranteed for the life of the carpet. If the cushion flattens out, the manufacturer will normally replace it.

TYPES OF PADDING

Yet with all the choices available, selecting the right carpet pad can be confusing. For this reason, a closer look at various types of padding will help you decide.

Hair and Jute Pads

The oldest type of underlay is the *hair and jute* pad, or *combination* pad (Fig. 5-1). This pad looks like thick felt and is made of a combination of pressed animal hair, usually cow or horse, blended with jute. It comes in 6- and 12-foot widths.

Fig. 5-1. Combination felt carpet pad.

A hair and jute pad provides the firmest *step* or feel, of all pads. It is sold by weight or thickness—from 32 ounces per square yard to around 80 ounces per square yard, and ⅜- to ¾-inch in thickness. It is particularly recommended under any type of woven carpet because it allows the carpet to stretch and flex the least.

Hair and jute pads are usually rubberized on one side to provide good adherence to the flooring, with the smooth side up to allow the carpet to slide over it during installation. If you are looking for a cushy feel under the carpet, this is not the right pad. Also, it is one of the higher-priced pads.

Rebond

The most commonly used pad is *rebond*, also known as bonded urethane (Fig. 5-2). It is made from recycled scrap foam and sponge rubber swept off the production lines of furniture makers and other foam users. The pieces are chopped into a uniform size and pressed together under pressure into huge "cakes," which are then sliced into the desired thickness. A plastic top sheet is often added to aid during installation by allowing the carpet to slide over it. The sheets are then rolled and wrapped. The finished product has a distinctive speckled color.

Rebond comes in several thicknesses (from ⅜ inch to ¾ inch) and densities (from 3 to 10 pounds per cubic foot), depending on the way you want it to feel under the carpet. The main objection to rebond seems to be lack of uniformity because of variation in materials. In fact, rebond works as well as any other pad given a

Fig. 5-2. Rebond carpet pad.

thick enough cushion for the type of traffic. Also, it does not flatten out in traffic areas any more than most other types of foam pads. Rebond is in the low to medium price range. A thicker rebond pad with low density will feel softer under the carpet than a thicker one with a high density.

Foam and Prime Urethane

Foam and *prime urethane* cushions are also popular. They are made by curing special aerated rubbers into blocks of foam. Prime urethane is made from high density foam, while regular foam is softer and less dense. The blocks are sliced into the desired thickness, with the sheets glued together to make rolls. Like rebond, foam and prime urethane are sold by density and thickness.

The important thing to remember when buying this type of pad is to check the pad's ability to keep the carpet from "bottoming out." Squeeze the sample between your fingers to see how much it will protect the carpet from the floor. The cheaper pads will squeeze to almost nothing. The better pads will compress to less than one-half—they will keep their buoyancy in high-traffic areas for the life of the carpet.

Foam and prime urethane cushions run the entire price range from low to high. Remember that low traffic areas such as bedrooms

Fig. 5-3. Rubber waffle carpet pad.

do not require thick pads, but that hallways and family rooms certainly do.

Another type of pad is the rubber waffle or "lump and bump," so called because of its bumpy appearance (Fig. 5-3). It is made by pouring aerated liquid rubber into molds. After cooling and curing, the sheets are joined and formed into rolls.

The best waffle pads are made with a high percentage of rubber. Unfortunately many are made with a great deal of filler material, usually clay, which can dry out and turn to powder in just a few years. The customer must depend on the dealer's integrity when choosing a quality waffle pad.

Waffle pad is sold by weight, ranging from 32 ounces per square yard up to 100 ounces per square yard. The 100-ounce cushion gives what has been described as an "executive feel" underfoot. Its main drawback is that fabrics can stretch severely after installation because of the extra flex afforded by the bumps in the pad.

Woven carpets should never be installed over a waffle pad, no matter what the configuration of the bumps or the weight of the pad. Carpets made with a non-woven primary or secondary backing should not be installed over the waffle pad, either. These types of backing need no extra flexing and work best over a smooth, firm pad.

MORE BENEFITS OF PADDING

Padding offers several other benefits besides longer-lasting carpet. Underlayments also add insulation to one's home. Carpet and padding increase the R-rating of wood floors. With today's heating bills, that can add up to a substantial savings.

In addition, carpet and pad reduce drafts by sealing gaps around baseboards and between floorboards. Noise and echo are reduced substantially, while safety increases because better footing is provided. This is why many hospitals and schools now install carpet instead of hard surfaced floors.

CHOOSING CARPET PADDING

The best way to choose a pad is to put your carpet selection on top of each of the better qualities of the various pads in order to see how each one feels underfoot. The final selection is a matter of personal preference as long as the pad is adequate for the traffic expected. Keep in mind that a good pad can make an average carpet look and perform better and can make a good carpet feel even thicker and more luxurious. Use the heaviest pad on steps and all high-traffic areas, lighter pads elsewhere.

What about double-padding—using two layers of pad to create an extra-cushy feel? Besides using twice as much pad as is needed, the extra thickness causes most carpet fabrics to stretch too much. This leads to wrinkling, buckling, and other installation problems.

When used on steps, however, double-padding can be beneficial. The carpet on the nose (edge) of the stair tread gets so much abrasion that even wear-guaranteed fabrics are excluded from the warranty when installed on steps. Double-padding eliminates most of the friction produced by the carpet rubbing against the stair. Some installers object to double-padding stairs because it involves a little more work. The end result is worth the extra effort, however. Insist on it, especially when using a low-density pad.

Some carpet is available with the pad attached. This type of floor covering is called rubber-, foam-, or sponge-backed carpet. It was originally found only on level-loop kitchen-type carpet; but, today, shags, short shags, and textured fabrics also come with attached pads.

These fabrics tend to fall into the lower price ranges and appeal mainly to the do-it-yourselfer who wants to install his own carpet without the problem of stretching it over a pad. The fabric is simply cut to fit the room measurements. Several types of foams and rubbers are used to make the attached backings. However, the purpose of the pad is to prevent abrasion with the floor, so the denser (not necessarily thicker) the attached pad, the better the performance of the carpet.

6

Buying Carpet

The best way to choose a retailer is through the grapevine. Ask your friends and acquaintances. A recommendation from a happy customer is the best advertising for any store. Many small firms are excellent but cannot afford splashy newspaper ads or large spreads in the local telephone book. They depend on their customers to spread the word for them.

CHOOSING A RETAILER

On the whole, however, you can buy carpet through four main sources: "trunk of the car" operations, interior designers, specialty floor covering stores, and department stores.

"Trunk of the Car" Operations

"Trunk of the car" generally refers to a one-person operation with a sales department that doubles as the installation crew. Materials are usually purchased through a local carpet distributor because the operation is too small to deal with most mills. Samples are kept in the trunk of a car, rather than in a showroom, and are shown in the home or on site.

While it is possible to get a great deal from a freelancer because of low overhead, buying from distributors can raise costs up to 30 percent. And while some freelancers offer other services, selection is smaller than in a large carpet department.

Freelancers are hard to locate because they do not have storefronts. In fact, about the only way to find a freelancer is a personal recommendation by an acquaintance. If you decide to work with one, by all means check references for experience and customer satisfaction. If workmanship is guaranteed and selection is reasonable, you could receive excellent personalized service right in your home.

Interior Designers

Calling in an interior designer is another alternative. The individual can range from a freelancer with an ASID (American Society of Interior Designers) certificate, to one working for the custom design studio in a major department store. Some designers are no more than salespeople; others might present a long list of impressive credentials. Some charge an hourly fee, while others work on commission only.

Yet all designers must fulfill certain requirements. To begin with, they must have good taste. This is something that is extremely difficult to teach someone yet is obviously important to the outcome of the job. Also, the designer must get along well with the client. Any friction will affect the final results. Ideally, the relationship should be like a friendship, with both sides placing ideas and input into the project.

Hiring an interior designer costs more than purchasing carpet from a department store, but a creative designer will have unusual sources and a wide selection. They can also help with more than just floor coverings and window treatments. Most items are special-ordered, adding to the cost. However, designers often create custom colors and designs for a truly individual touch.

Specialty Stores

Stores specializing in carpets and area rugs are quickly gaining popularity. Many offer window treatments and hard-surface flooring, as well. In smaller operations, the owner of the store usually does the buying, deciding what the local clientele would like. He also sells the carpeting and is often knowledgeable because he deals with salespeople from the mills and travels to trade shows.

In larger specialty stores, a staff of decorators takes care of these functions. A large carpet store will have a well-stocked selection of styles and qualities purchased from three to six main suppliers, and more from "special order" mills or distributors. Buying directly from a mill results in lower costs to the store. Large-volume stores that buy full rolls and stock them in their own warehouse realize the most savings. Buying small cuts or parts of rolls is an expensive way to purchase materials.

Mills also contribute to advertising budgets for the larger operations. Effective advertising can help sell a lot of extra carpet. Many specialty stores offer shop-at-home services, too.

Department Stores

Department stores are the traditional purveyors of rugs and carpeting. They generally offer a wide-ranging carpet department with experienced salespeople. Some offer a separate interior design studio. Selection is large, with the store's buyer determining the lines and stock items.

Most department stores subcontract the installation to carpet workshops, but usually the workroom is just an extension of the store. Department stores rely heavily on customer satisfaction and bend over backwards to correct problems. Many department stores belong to buying groups that pool their money to buy en masse and receive the lowest possible prices from the mills. This could lead to a lack of variety among department stores, but the buyer adds to the basic selection and accounts for local tastes.

Department stores often conduct seminars for the staff to keep them updated and informed. Frequently, mills or yarn suppliers host technical movies and lectures for a carpet department. Large mills have been known to fly in entire carpet departments for extensive tours demonstrating manufacturing techniques. Naturally, only their best customers receive this type of treatment.

SHOPPING WISELY

If you study carpet ads in the newspaper, you'll discover that, although carpet stores have sales every week of the year, the best time to buy is in the early spring or fall of each year. At these times the buyers have returned from the seasonal markets and shows. They have seen the latest styles and have made their major purchases or commitments for the current season. Mills offer market specials on introductory lines or established winners, which are passed along to consumers as major specials.

Carpet ads also give a general idea about the price range you can expect to find—from too cheap to believe to outrageously expensive. What causes such great differences in price? Obviously, quality accounts for most of the price spreads. The better the carpet, the more one can expect to pay for it. But other factors are involved.

Mills frequently give better prices to big buyers, antitrust laws notwithstanding. The dealer can then pass the savings along to you. Large department stores are often members of huge buying groups. A chain store, or many chain stores, buy together in volume to get the lowest possible price from a mill. The selection is frequently limited to a few selected styles, but the savings to the consumer is great.

Even "trunk of the car" salespeople can offer a low price by practically giving away the carpet in order to make their profit by installing the carpet themselves. Independent retailers can also join buying groups to lower their wholesale price. While no one has yet developed a generic carpet to lower prices further, volume buying definitely results in savings for everyone.

Other ways for a dealer to lower the net cost include reducing shipping costs. By combining several small shipments all going to the same general destination into one large group, retailers realize substantial savings when measured over several months. These savings are frequently passed on to consumers. The carpet rolls are delivered to a central location where the individual stores pick up their orders.

Buying directly from a mill as opposed to a local distributor saves between 20 and 30 percent. First, the dealer must promise volume purchases, at least of selected patterns and colors. The mill is assured of a certain volume when combined with orders from all over the country. Also, the mill can plan a long run of these patterns, thereby lowering its production costs by buying yarns and dyes in large lots. Mills will frequently warehouse the finished goods for dealers, reducing costs and taxes for the dealer.

Another means of cost-cutting is available to the astute retailer. By buying mill trials and seconds (irregulars), carpet shops can realize substantial savings. Some people find these methods distasteful because the goods are not considered first quality. However, all areas must be considered if the retailer wants to save money.

Mill trials often *are* first-quality merchandise. Frequently, mills experiment with new patterns or new colorations of old patterns. While something might look good on graph paper, only a production run will show the fabric as the consumer sees it. The mill might make several rolls of the new pattern only to find that it is not as popular in the marketplace as they had hoped, so they sell it to dealers at a special price.

Seconds or irregulars are a different story. Many factors can create an irregular. The finished product might be a shade different than the sample but is still up to first-quality standards in every other way. The roll might contain streaks or color variations. The heat-set might not be perfect. Another possibility is that the secondary backing might not be properly adhered.

Anything that keeps a roll of carpet from being perfect makes it a second. However, any reputable dealer who sells irregulars will cull the worst rolls from stock, advise the consumer that the carpet is an irregular, and allow an inspection of the roll by the customer to ensure that the irregularity apparent in the roll is the only thing wrong with the carpet.

Irregulars generally carry no warranty by the mill and are sold "as is." The savings can be substantial, however. Buying an irregular for certain installations—such as a guest bedroom or rental property—might be a good alternative.

THROUGH THE CARPET STORES

Now, considering color, quality, and price, let's go shopping. We will visit an imaginary carpet shop together, actually a composite of the stores one is likely to encounter. As we walk through the doors, we are greeted by a carpet specialist who is eager to help us with our selection. We tell our salesperson we are only looking at this point. He suggests we look around and familiarize ourselves with the store, then come to him with any questions or requests.

Having a competent salesperson helps make the purchase and installation of carpeting a much easier task. When choosing a particular decorator or salesperson, you must keep in mind that personality is a key factor. The decorator-consumer relationship should be like friends working together, easy-going and comfortable. The decorator or salesperson should not be too pushy or aggressive and should help guide the decision-making.

Of course, knowledge of the product is also important. If the explanations you receive are vague or confusing, consider talking to someone else—someone who knows what he is selling and explains things simply and clearly. Also, look at the sales presentation. A reputable dealer has nothing to hide. He is eager to explain his goods and services and wouldn't think about selling one product to you and delivering something else—the old bait and switch trick. He knows his carpets in detail and is proud of his store. And remember one other thing. Most salespeople work on commission. Why give a lot of money to someone you dislike or distrust?

As we look around at the store, we see an enormous selection in every color of the rainbow. Some goods are in stock and are ready for immediate delivery and installation. Other patterns must be special-ordered and take six to eight weeks for delivery. The selection could be terribly confusing, but because we have already decided upon a certain color and price range, our choices will automatically be reduced.

Let's assume that we want a particular shade of green. No matter what the common name is, carpet mills have thought up dozens of other descriptive names for the same color, such as Jungle Grass, Ocean, or even Special Green. It is easiest when selecting a color to bring along a swatch of upholstery or drapery fabric that you want to match with your carpet. Ideally, the best way to color scheme is to select your carpet first and design the rest of the room around this basic color. Of course, you cannot always start from the floor up, especially when you have a favorite sofa or accent piece you are trying to match.

Some shops group each color together, so that all shades are easy to find. Some stores keep all the colors of each pattern or quality together so that you can see a complete selection. No matter what the store layout, finding the correct shade among the rainbow of colors presented is relatively easy. More difficult to find is the correct quality and fiber type, as carpets are available in such a wide variety of fibers and blends as well as varying weights and thicknesses.

Labels

The labels found on the backs of carpet samples are very informative and helpful when making a carpet selection. Samples have at least one label, and some have several. Let's look at some labels and get an idea of what they explain.

The label shown in Fig. 6-1 identifies the manufacturer, gives the name of the pattern and color, and identifies the fabric content as nylon fiber. The biggest help to us is knowing the fiber content. Based on what we know about fibers and their characteristics, we can decide if this pattern will work well for our needs. Most mills make a wide assortment of qualities, with prices to match. Besides, many mills "private label" their goods by putting only the retailer's house brand on the label (Fig. 6-2).

Picking another sample from a different rack, we find several labels. In addition to the ones stating fiber content and quality name, another identifies the backing material (Fig. 6-3). This one happens

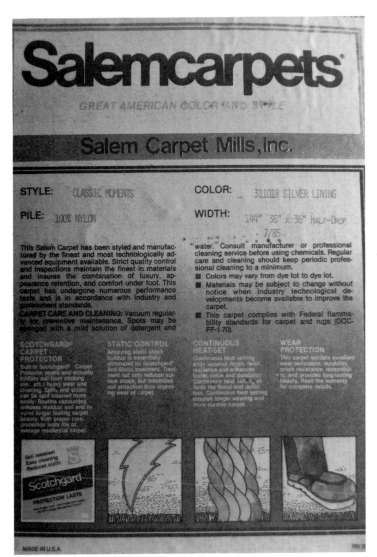

Fig. 6-1. A carpet sample label that shows the carpet mill name, style, pile fiber, color, and width.

to explain the advantages of a branded synthetic backing, Action-Bac, made by Amoco Fabrics Co., but it could just as well have explained the advantages of a jute backing. Actually, the secondary backing isn't too important to the average customer, unless moisture is a factor, such as in a damp basement. Then synthetic backings

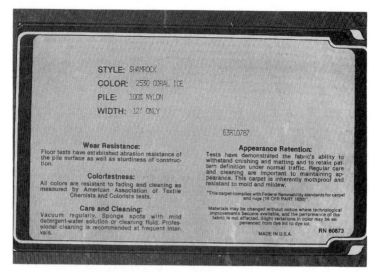

STYLE: SHAMROCK

COLOR: 2530 CORAL ICE

PILE: 100% NYLON

WIDTH: 12' ONLY

63R1.0787

Wear Resistance:
Floor tests have established abrasion resistance of the pile surface as well as sturdiness of construction.

Colorfastness:
All colors are resistant to fading and cleaning as measured by American Association of Textile Chemists and Colorists tests.

Care and Cleaning:
Vacuum regularly. Sponge spots with mild detergent-water solution or cleaning fluid. Professional cleaning is recommended at frequent intervals.

Appearance Retention:
Tests have demonstrated the fabric's ability to withstand crushing and matting and to retain pattern definition under normal traffic. Regular care and cleaning are important to maintaining appearance. This carpet is inherently mothproof and resistant to mold and mildew.

"This carpet complies with Federal flammability standards for carpet and rugs (16 CFR PART 1630)".

Materials may be changed without notice where technological improvements become available, and the performance of the fabric is not affected. Slight variations in color may be experienced from dye lot to dye lot.

MADE IN U.S.A.

RN 60873

Fig. 6-2. A "private label" carpet sample.

have an advantage over jute because the synthetics won't support mold growth.

A more helpful label is the one that explains the face yarn, which is the fiber that is walked on after the carpet is installed. In this case, the label tells about Ultron (Fig. 6-4), a nylon fiber from Monsanto Corporation. We find another that explains Antron nylon (Fig. 6-5), made by Du Pont, and a third one explains Anso IV (Fig. 6-6), made by Allied Corporation. The labels explain how these advanced-generation nylons resist soil and stains due to a protector built into the molecular structure of the yarn. This means that topically applied soil retardants such as Scotchgard or Teflon are not necessary for these fabrics to perform well. (Some manufacturers like to put them on their carpets anyway.)

Anti-static qualities are also built in. Static electricity was a big problem for the early nylons, but the advanced generation yarns have eliminated it. All these features help the carpet keep its new look longer.

Still another label explains that the yarns are heat-set (Fig. 6-7.) This is very important because it means that the cut, plied yarns will keep their twist through usage and cleaning, and will maintain the original appearance much better than yarns which are not heat-set. (Looped fabrics are not always heat-set because they cannot untwist.) This process bakes the twist memory into the yarn and prevents premature texture change and matting.

Fig. 6-3. A label explaining Action-Bac brand secondary backing.

Most people equate severe change in texture with wear. When a carpet is fuzzy and flat, it looks worn out, even if the face pile has not actually worn away to the backing. Most yarns today are heat-set. But there are many methods used; some work better than others. The actual type of heat-set used in a particular fabric is often impossible to determine. The consumer must hope that the mill has used an adequate method. Most do.

There is no sure-fire way to see if the heat-set is good. You can take a single tuft, untwist it by rolling between your fingers, and see if the tuft returns to its original shape. Some tufts can take more of this test than others, indicating the relative degree of heat-set.

Another test is to look closely at the tightness of the twist (Fig. 6-8). Naturally, the "hardness" of the twist will vary depending on

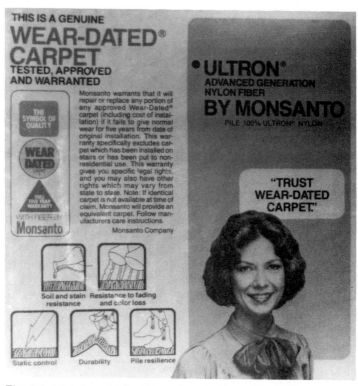

Fig. 6-4. A label explaining Ultron brand advanced-generation nylon by Monsanto.

the look that the original designer had in mind. In general, tightly twisted tufts do not look fuzzy or distorted on the cut tips. The tufts are twisted to the ends with no flare at the tips. The twist is even throughout both plies of yarn, with little fuzziness. Twist and heat-set are important to the long life of all cut-pile carpets.

Because the pattern we are looking at is a cut-pile, we see another label that states that shading and pile reversal are normal for these fabrics (Fig. 6-9). It is important to remember that cut-piles show footprints and vacuum cleaner wheel marks. The longer the pile, the more they show. Cut-piles also show color variation, similar to crushed velvet upholstery, caused by areas of carpet piles reversing direction. This is normal for any cut-pile. The amount varies according to the individual fabric.

Some people find shading to be a pleasant effect. Others mistakenly see it as a defect. Consumers should be aware that a

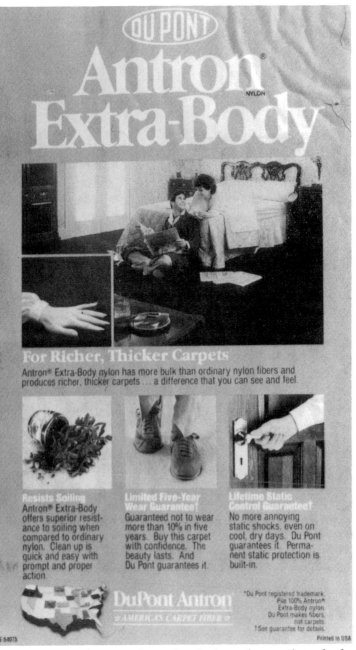

Fig. 6-5. *A label explaining Antron brand advanced-generation nylon by Du Pont.*

Fig. 6-6. A label explaining Anso IV brand advanced-generation nylon by Allied Corp.

considerable amount of shading could turn up in any carpet and should decide ahead of time if this condition is desirable.

Yet another label identifies the yarn as BCF nylon. This refers to bulked continuous filament nylon, or the non-shedding type. As you rub the sample and tug gently on the yarn ends, you will notice very little fluff or shed. This is very different from the first sample

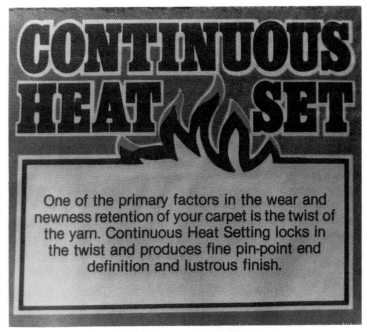

Fig. 6-7. Label showing this pattern has heat-set yarns.

Fig. 6-8. A drawing that shows the difference between tightly twisted yarn and loosely twisted yarn.

that fuzzed a lot when rubbed. Even though the label doesn't state it, the pile must be a staple fiber. This is important because some people don't want to have a new carpet that fuzzes a lot or forms a lot of lint. While any carpet should be vacuumed frequently and thoroughly, staple fabrics need more maintenance.

Most people don't realize that all carpet is tested for smoke and flammability, according to minimum federal government standards. Residential carpet does not have to pass the test, but ones that do usually have a label stating the fact. The testing is a long and expensive process for the mills.

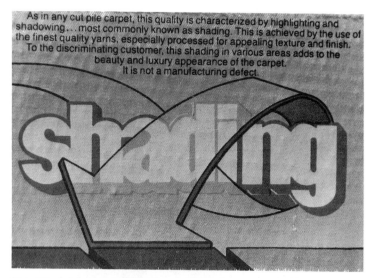

As in any cut pile carpet, this quality is characterized by highlighting and shadowing... most commonly known as shading. This is achieved by the use of the finest quality yarns, especially processed for appealing texture and finish. To the discriminating customer, this shading in various areas adds to the beauty and luxury appearance of the carpet. It is not a manufacturing defect.

Fig. 6-9. A label explaining the condition known as shading.

Another label explains the 5-year wear warranty that comes with this particular fabric (Fig. 6-10). Because this carpet meets certain quality standards, it is warranted by the mill and fiber producer not to lose more than 20 percent of the face yarn in five years. The carpet will be replaced free if testing shows a loss greater than 20 percent in any area. What this means to you is that the carpet will not wear to the backing any time soon. It is the best statement a mill can make regarding its product.

Even though you are not interested in patterned carpet, let's check the labels of one just for fun. The carpet is a woven Axminster. One label (Fig. 6-11) contains information about the weave, fiber content (note that this is a blend), and pattern match, as well as cleaning and ''fitting'' instructions. We also see that the carpet is made in England and passes their flammability tests. Another label on this carpet cautions about pattern match, the use of chair pads, and pattern lines (Fig. 6-12).

When you walk into a showroom area that contains wool broadloom, you will find some samples are woven and others are tufted. Each sample containing wool has a label with the Woolmark identifying it as containing 100 percent wool pile (Fig. 6-13). It further explains that this quality holds up under heavy residential use. Another label explains the colors and irregularities inherent to wool berber carpet, and that these irregularities are part of a natural fi-

The manufacturer warrants that if any area of this carpet wears more than 20% due to fiber lost from carpet within 5 years, the carpet will be replaced at manufacturer's expense provided the carpet is properly installed and maintained, and is used for indoor residential use only. Carpet on stairs is excluded from this warranty, and this warranty covers abrasion wear only and not tears, pulls, cuts, piling, shedding or matting. For warranty service contact Salem Carpet Mills, Inc., P.O. Box 12429, Winston-Salem, N.C. 27107. This warranty gives you specific legal rights, and you may have other rights which vary from state to state.

Fig. 6-10. A label explaining a carpet's 5-year residential wear warranty.

Fig. 6-11. A label explaining an Axminster weave pattern, including fiber content, pattern match, cleaning, and installing instructions.

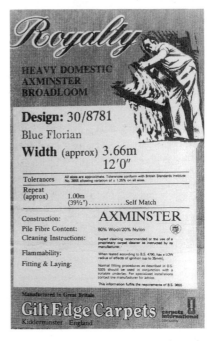

53

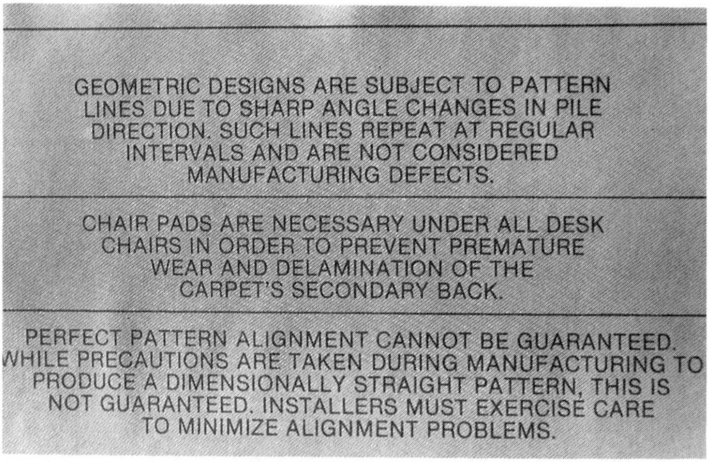

GEOMETRIC DESIGNS ARE SUBJECT TO PATTERN
LINES DUE TO SHARP ANGLE CHANGES IN PILE
DIRECTION. SUCH LINES REPEAT AT REGULAR
INTERVALS AND ARE NOT CONSIDERED
MANUFACTURING DEFECTS.

CHAIR PADS ARE NECESSARY UNDER ALL DESK
CHAIRS IN ORDER TO PREVENT PREMATURE
WEAR AND DELAMINATION OF THE
CARPET'S SECONDARY BACK.

PERFECT PATTERN ALIGNMENT CANNOT BE GUARANTEED.
WHILE PRECAUTIONS ARE TAKEN DURING MANUFACTURING TO
PRODUCE A DIMENSIONALLY STRAIGHT PATTERN, THIS IS
NOT GUARANTEED. INSTALLERS MUST EXERCISE CARE
TO MINIMIZE ALIGNMENT PROBLEMS.

Fig. 6-12. A label with precautionary instructions.

ber (Fig. 6-14). The last label on this sample explains wool's
excellence as a carpet fiber (Fig. 6-15).

If all this seems bewildering, take heart! You are now ready to
discuss color, style, and quality with a trained decorator. Just work
with someone likable and knowledgeable, and you will enjoy the
choices which are ahead of you. Then, after the selection has been
made and the carpet of your choice is installed, you can sit back and
relax in the comfort of your newly improved home.

Fig. 6-13. A label explaining wool carpet and exhibiting the Woolmark (pure wool).

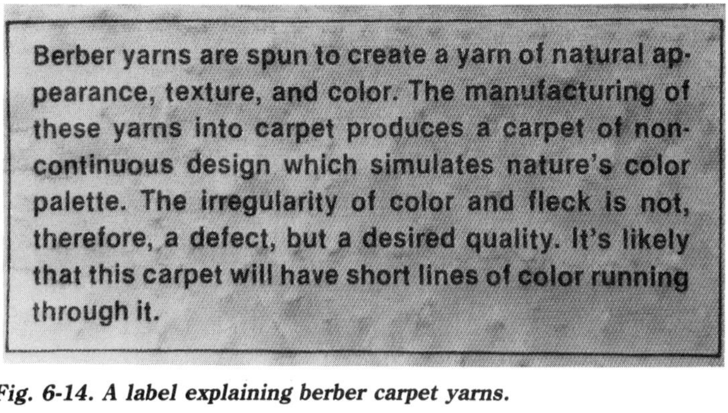

Berber yarns are spun to create a yarn of natural appearance, texture, and color. The manufacturing of these yarns into carpet produces a carpet of noncontinuous design which simulates nature's color palette. The irregularity of color and fleck is not, therefore, a defect, but a desired quality. It's likely that this carpet will have short lines of color running through it.

Fig. 6-14. A label explaining berber carpet yarns.

WHY WOOL?

Wool is Warm

You feel warmer with wool when
it's cold outside because wool is warmer.
Tests show wool carpet can cut heat loss by 13%.

Wool is Cool

When air conditioning is on, wool keeps you cooler
because it absorbs moisture and stays cool to the touch.

Wool Resists Fire

Drop a burning cigarette on wool and watch.
Wool will not support combustion.
The cold ash can be swept away.

Wool is Durable

The resilience lasts and lasts.
Wool retains its appearance longer than any synthetic.

Wool is Tough

Leave a piece of furniture on a wool carpet
and move it months - even years later.
The fiber restores itself.

Wool is Neat

Wool cleans better and won't soil quickly. Why?
Because wool resists oily air-borne grime
and can wash out completely without a residue.
Synthetics simply can't.

 . . . GOOD LOOKS THAT LAST

Fig. 6-15. A label explaining wool's good points and exhibiting the Woolmark (pure wool).

7

Carpet Installation

Now we come to an area which is almost ignored during the purchase of carpeting: the installation of your new carpet in your home. Practically all broadloom is laid wall-to-wall over the pad. Some is glued directly to the floor (as with kitchen carpet), and occasionally the carpet is cut and bound into loose area rugs. Whether you are installing the carpet yourself or having it professionally installed, the information in this chapter is vital to the durability and performance of your new carpet. Remember, the quality of the installation is as important as the quality of the carpet.

DO-IT-YOURSELF INSTALLATION

Do-it-yourself carpet installation is probably one of the most difficult projects a person can undertake. Anything more than a single room can turn into a nightmare. Tools are specialized and difficult to find at most rental stores. Laying tackstrip is technically more difficult than it looks (Fig. 7-1). Seaming is troublesome even for professional installers. And, of course, stretching the carpet properly over the pad can be backbreaking.

Do-it-yourself installation is definitely for the stout-hearted. It is for these individuals that I give installation instructions. Here are the most important points to know about an installation, whether over pad or glued down.

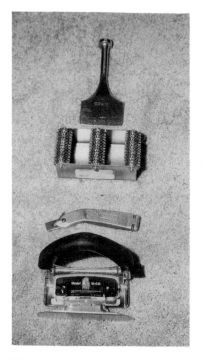

Fig. 7-1. Carpet tools: (top) stair tool, (top center) seam tractor, (bottom center) carpet knife, (bottom) edge trimmer.

Measuring

First it is necessary to accurately measure the areas you will carpet. This is not as easy as it sounds. Most carpet comes in standard 12-foot widths, but many rooms are wider than 12 feet. You cannot measure a room, take length times width, and come up with the correct square footage, then convert it into square yards. It is necessary to take waste carpet from rooms narrower than 12 feet and apply the extra fabric to the rooms that are greater than 12 feet or cut the needed carpet from the end of the roll, as is explained later in the chapter.

Careful measuring will help you determine where the seams will go. You should make a seam diagram and study it. Placement of the seams is important because seamed areas usually are among the first places to show wear. Therefore, seams should be placed in areas with little use whenever possible. In addition, how the installation is seamed determines how much carpet is needed to complete the job. You don't want to come up several yards short!

Most rooms can be laid out in two directions. One way uses fewer seams and more waste. The other uses more seams and less waste. Since most jobs laid out with minimum seaming only use a

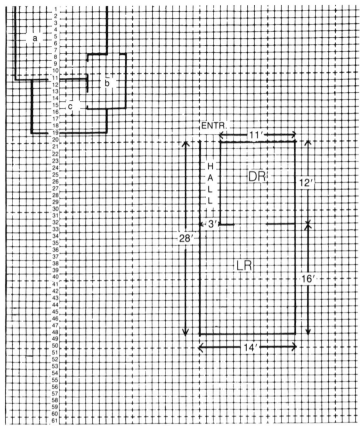

Fig. 7-2. A floor plan showing all room measurements.

few extra yards of material, most people choose to have a little extra scrap rather than more seams.

In our example (Fig. 7-2), two rooms and a hall are measured for installation and are laid out on graph paper to keep proportions and measurements accurate. The living room is 14 feet wide and 16 feet long. The dining room is 11 feet wide and 12 feet long, with a 3-foot-wide and 12-foot-long hall next to it. The total width of 14 feet is multiplied by the total length of 28 feet, for a total figure of 392 square feet. Dividing this figure by 9 gives the square yards, which is 43.5. This figure is not necessarily the amount you need to order. Because the total job is wider than the 12-foot width of the carpet, it is necessary to calculate the fill pieces and waste into the total figure.

To have enough carpet to do the job neatly, you must start with

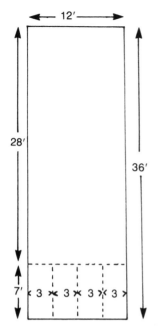

Fig. 7-3. Cutting 12-foot-wide carpet to fit a 14-foot-wide room.

a piece 12 feet × 36 feet (Fig. 7-3). This totals 48 square yards. Cutting a piece 12 × 28 feet, 6 inches gives enough to cover the full length of all three areas, with a piece 12 × 7 feet, 6 inches left for cutting into the 3 × 7 feet, 6 inch pieces needed to fill in the room (Fig. 7-4). There is just enough carpet to provide a little extra in case the room is not square.

Once you have decided on the layout, the correct amount of fabric and pad is ordered and delivered. Then the actual physical installation begins. You must first remove the old carpet and pad, if necessary. If you are installing the carpet over a pad (as opposed to gluing it down), and the room has never had wall-to-wall carpet in it, begin by placing tackless-strip (commonly referred to as simply tackstrip) all around the room perimeters, including floor vents (Figs. 7-5, 7-6). Stairs are also tack-stripped (Fig. 7-7).

Putting Down Tackstrip

The function of tackstrip is to provide a smooth, tight installation, without unsightly dimples around the edges caused by nailing tacks or shooting staples into the carpet and floor. The strips are prenailed with two to four rows of gripper pins set at a 60-degree angle. The 4-foot lengths are nailed to wood floors and glued or nailed to concrete. They are lightweight and are easily trimmed for tight areas

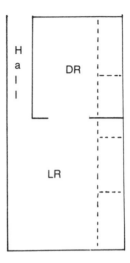

Fig. 7-4. A seam diagram for Fig. 7-3 floor plan. Dotted lines indicate seams.

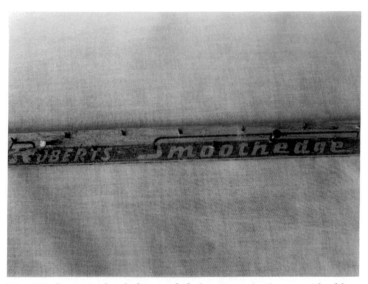

Fig. 7-5. Carpet tackstrip has angled pins that grip the carpet backing.

or upholstery work. The carpet is stretched over the pad, then hooked and held by gripper pins.

It is not always wise to use old tackstrip when replacing old carpet. The strip is laid away from the wall according to the thickness of the carpet. If the total thickness of the carpet is ¾ inch, for example, the strip is laid ½ inch away from the wall (Fig. 7-8). If the old carpet was quite different in thickness from what you plan

Fig. 7-6. Tackstrip around floor vents.

to install, the new carpet might not wedge between the strip and wall properly, and the carpet might not stay stretched on the tackstrip pins. If the strip is in good condition and is the correct distance from the wall, it is perfectly all right to use it. Double rows of strip are used if the carpet is put over extra thick pad, if the carpet will get extra heavy use, or if it is installed over a concrete floor (Fig. 7-9).

Fig. 7-7. Tackstrip steps at the bottom of the riser and the back of the tread.

One other fact is necessary to consider when using old tackstrip. The gripper pins come in different lengths, depending on the thickness and type of carpet backing. It is possible for long pins to go through relatively thin carpet, causing punctured toes when walking barefoot.

Pad

Once the tackstrip is installed, the pad is laid down (Fig. 7-10). Most pad comes in 4- or 6-foot widths, or drops, with two or three drops equalling one width of the carpet. The drops should be as close together as possible, using the fewest possible cuts. They are stapled to wood floors and glued to concrete to prevent the pad from shifting (Fig. 7-11). Seams can be taped to create a completely smooth surface. Then the pad is trimmed against the tackstrip.

Carpet seams should not lay over the pad seams. Most pads have a smooth or slippery surface on one side only. This is the "up" side, and the slick surface allows the carpet backing to slide smoothly over the pad when you stretch the carpet. You have now completed the easiest part of the installation.

Most people agree that the most important part of the installation is the cutting, seaming, and stretching of the carpet itself. You need

Fig. 7-8. The carpet fits between the tackstrip and the wall.

Fig. 7-9. Double rows of tackstrip around a curve.

specialized tools for this part of the undertaking, as well as skill and patience, to complete this part of the installation.

Carpet is made in long rolls, often 100 feet or more. Today the standard width is 12 feet, although a carpet as narrow as 11 feet, 10 inches meets the minimum standard. As determined by the seam diagram, cut the correct amount from the roll in one piece. If more than one roll is needed, the consecutive dye lots (rolls all of the same

Fig. 7-10. Padding the steps.

dye run) are called for. Professional installers often do preliminary cutting in a large workroom or warehouse, and bring the partially cut roll to the job site for final cutting and fitting. Most do-it-yourselfers do not have the luxury of a workroom and will do their cutting in a driveway or yard.

Cutting the Carpet

It is most important to make clean, straight cuts, usually from the back of the carpet through to the front. A straight edge made from a long, flat aluminum strip helps with the task. When cutting

Fig. 7-11. Attaching the pad to the floor.

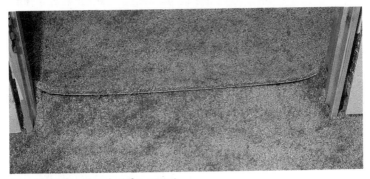

Fig. 7-12. Overlapping the carpet.

and seaming carpet, extra fabric is allowed for overlaps of a couple of inches along the walls and seams, which are later trimmed away (Fig. 7-12). This prevents you from coming up short when the pieces are put together. This also shows why you cannot measure a room down to the last inch, and why you must figure waste into the final measurement. Cut all carpet according to your seam diagram and lay the pieces out in their correct places.

A word of caution is needed here. All fabric, including carpet, has a sweep or direction in which the nap lays. When piecing carpet together, it is *most* important to be sure all pieces lay in the same direction.

It is easy to determine the lay of the nap of most carpets. It either lays up or down the length of the roll. Take your hand and brush the pile first in one lengthwise direction, then the other. You will notice that the pile seems to stand up or lay down depending on which way you brush it. Up makes the color look darker. Down makes the color look lighter.

Stair carpeting should go with the nap running down the steps. Otherwise, it doesn't really matter which way you lay the nap in a room. The important thing to remember is that when you seam pieces together, either in between two rooms or when adding fill pieces to one room, you must always lay the carpet so the nap of all pieces runs in the same direction. If you do not follow this rule, the pieces will look like they are different colors when seamed together.

It's easy to keep yourself from installing pieces the wrong way. After each piece is cut from the roll, draw an arrow on the back of the piece with a magic marker indicating the pile direction. When you lay out the pieces before seaming, check the back of each piece and make sure the arrows are all pointing in the same direction.

All rows of carpet, whether woven or tufted, have a selvedge along each side that must be trimmed away. The *selvedge* is a raw edge of unfilled backing material which extends beyond the normal width of the carpet. Some mills trim off the selvedge before delivering the finished carpet, some do not. If your carpet still has the selvedge attached, you must trim it off in order to be able to seam the carpet along the sides, known as side seaming. (Seams made across the 12-foot width are called cross seams.)

Once the carpet is trimmed, cut to size, and laid out in the proper areas, it is ready for seaming. Carpet seams may be either hand sewn or hot-melt taped, also called *hot-taping* or *hot-seaming*. It is highly preferable to hand sew all woven goods, while tufted fabrics seam well whether hand sewn or hot-taped.

Seaming Woven Carpet

Many woven fabrics ravel badly along any cut edge, including edges along walls, so you must apply a thin coat of latex rubber along all cut edges to seal them and prevent ravelling. The carpet is now ready for seaming. The two pieces to be joined are turned backside up and are cross-stitched together at three to four stitches per inch using a straight needle and waxed linen thread (Fig. 7-13).

Begin sewing in the center and work towards the outside. Care must be taken not to catch any face yarns in the stitching or they will be pulled down and make holes along the seam. The same seam sealer that was applied to the room perimeters is applied to the cut

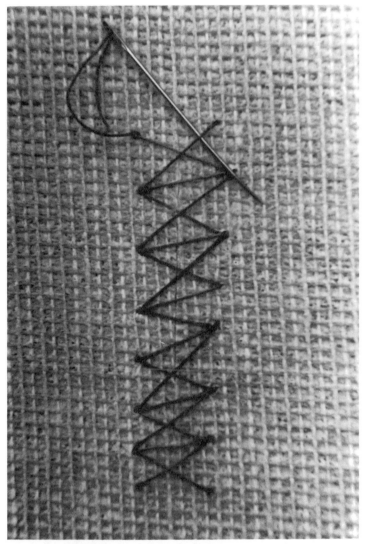

Fig. 7-13. A hand-sewn cross-stitched seam.

edges of the seam, using a needle-nosed squeeze bottle. This bonds the separate pieces of fabric into a solid sheet. As additional protection against premature wear, latex is put over the linen stitching itself. When all seaming is completed, the carpet is turned over and is stretched in over the tackstrip using a knee kicker (Fig. 7-14) and power stretcher (Fig. 7-15). The stretching sequence differs depending on the type of woven carpet used.

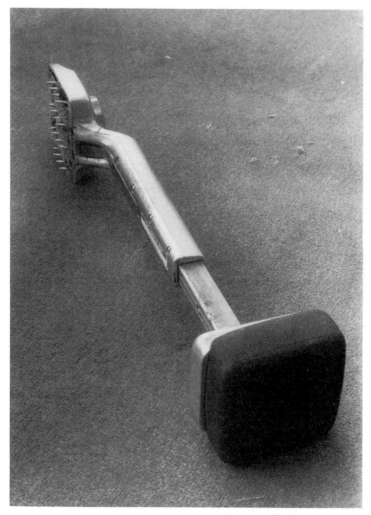

Fig. 7-14. A knee kicker showing the toothed head and knee pad.

Fig. 7-15. A power stretcher with extension tubes across the room.

Using the Knee Kicker

The head of the knee kicker is placed a few inches from the wall. The knee kicker uses gripper teeth to slide the carpet over the tackstrip along the walls. When the kicker is removed from the carpet, the carpet gets hooked on the angled pins of the tackstrip as it slides backwards.

The teeth of the kicker are adjusted for the thickness of the carpet. If the teeth are set too deeply, they snag the padding and the carpet doesn't slide. If the teeth are not set deeply enough, they do not grip the backing and can tear it. Kicker tears result when the face yarns fall out of the torn backing. Instead, the teeth are adjusted so that they grip the backing without breaking it.

The kicker is gripped by the neck behind the head and downward pressure is applied to the head while the kicker pad is bumped using the leg just above the knee. As the kicker head moves over the tackstrip, the downward pressure pushes the carpet back and onto the gripper pins of the tackstrip. A stair tool or hammer head slid over the carpet pile pushes it firmly onto the pins. This causes the overlap to stick up at a 90-degree angle above the gully between the tackstrip and the wall. A stair tool or other wide blade is used to tuck the overlap into the gully (Fig. 7-16). This holds the carpet fast while it is stretched.

71

Fig. 7-16. Stretching, hooking, and tucking the carpet.

Using the Power Stretcher

Like the knee kicker, the power stretcher also has a head containing adjustable teeth. The power stretcher's tubes are extended so that the head is about 3 inches away from the wall onto which the carpet is being stretched (Fig. 7-17). A power stretcher moves a carpet about 1 inch per 10 feet of carpet length. (This figure varies with the type construction and quality of the carpet.)

As the handle is slowly pumped a few times, the carpet stretches across the room (Fig. 7-18). When the handle is locked, the carpet

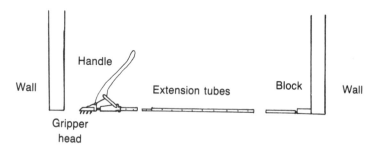

Fig. 7-17. A power stretcher.

Fig. 7-18. Pumping the power stretcher handle.

is held in place (Fig. 7-19). The knee kicker holds the carpet down behind the tackstrip while the stretcher handle is raised. This releases the pressure from the stretcher head and the carpet pulls back and down onto the tackstrip pins.

Practice using the knee kicker and power stretcher before the actual installation. A little practice goes a long way towards making a better, easier installation for you.

Stretching Wilton and Velvet Weaves. Wilton and velvet weave carpets have a soft backing and can be stretched in any direction. To stretch in Wilton and velvet carpet, begin by anchoring the carpet on the tackstrip at corner A (Fig. 7-20). Then power stretch from A and hook the carpet to corner B. Using straight kicks with the knee kicker, hook the carpet along the width A to B. Then power stretch along wall A to C and hook the carpet onto the tackstrip at corner C. Again use straight kicks to hook the carpet along the length from A to C (Fig. 7-21).

Next, position the block end of the power stretcher against wall A-B 2 or 3 feet from corner B. The stretcher head is placed in corner D and the carpet is power stretched at a 15-degree angle and hooked in corner D (Fig. 7-22). Put the block of the stretcher in corner A and the head in corner B. Begin the power stretch here and move down the room using straight stretches every 2 to 3 feet, from wall A-B to wall C-D.

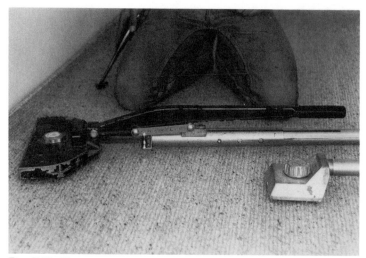

Fig. 7-19. The power stretcher locks in place.

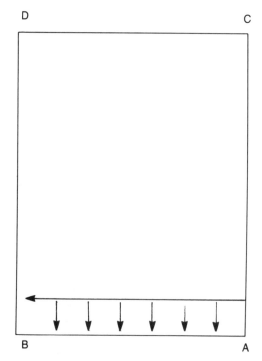

Fig. 7-20. Installing Wilton and velvet weave carpet. Step one. Power stretch from corner A to corner B and hook. Use straight knee kicks to hook carpet onto wall A–B.

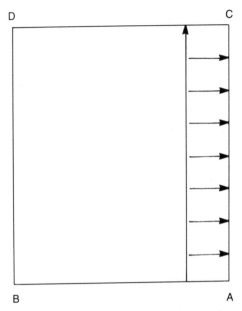

Fig. 7-21. Installing Wilton and velvet weave carpet. Step two. Power stretch from corner A to C and hook. Use straight knee kicks to hook carpet onto wall A-C.

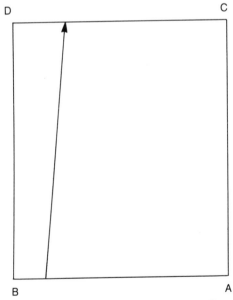

Fig. 7-22. Installing Wilton and velvet weave carpet. Step three. Power stretch from corner B at a 15-degree angle to corner D and hook.

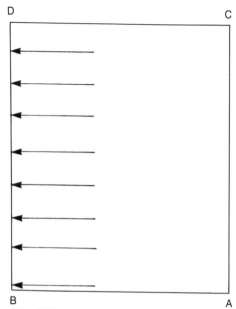

Fig. 7-23. Installing Wilton and velvet weave carpet. Step four. Use straight power stretches from wall A–C to hook carpet along wall B–D.

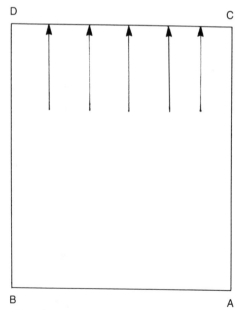

Fig. 7-24. Installing Wilton and velvet weave carpet. Step five. Use straight power stretches from wall B–A to hook the carpet along wall D–C.

76

Hook the carpet onto the tackstrip after each power stretch (Fig. 7-23). Returning to corner A, place the block of the stretcher here and the head of the stretcher in corner C. Stretching the length of the carpet along the wall A-B every 2 or 3 feet hooks the carpet onto the tackstrip of wall C-D (Fig. 7-24). The carpet is now completely stretched in.

Stretching Axminster Carpet. Axminster carpet is the only one that just stretches lengthwise, so it is stretched differently from

Fig. 7-25. The patterned pile of an Axminster weave carpet.

the other constructions. It is easy to recognize because the pattern is woven through the back (Figs. 7-25, 7-26). Begin by anchoring the carpet in corner A (see Fig. 7-27). Put the block of the stretcher in corner A and the head in corner C. Power stretch the length from A to C and hook the carpet on the tackstrip at corner C. Then straight kick along wall A-C to hook the carpet on the tackstrip along this wall.

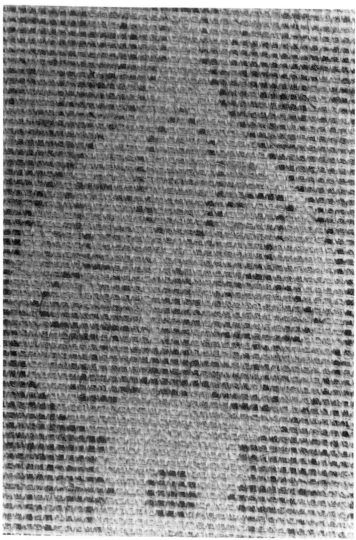

Fig. 7-26. The Axminster pattern is woven through the back.

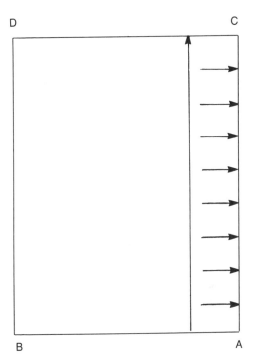

Fig. 7-27. Installing Axminster weave carpet. Step one. Power stretch from corner A to corner C and hook the carpet. Use straight knee kicks along wall A-C and hook the carpet.

Next use the kicker to stretch and hook the carpet onto the tackstrip at corner B. Using straight kicks, hook the carpet onto the tackstrip along wall A-B (Fig. 7-28). Follow this by placing the stretcher block in corner B and, putting the head in corner D, power stretch the entire length of wall B-D and hook the carpet to the tackstrip in corner D (Fig. 7-29). Then put the block of the stretcher in corner A and the head in corner C.

Power stretch the length of the carpet, hooking the carpet to the tackstrip along wall C-D. Move the block of the stretcher every 2 or 3 feet along wall A-B and stretch along the entire wall C-D, hooking the carpet on the tackstrip pins as you go (Fig. 7-30). Use straight kicks with the knee kicker along the entire wall B-D and hook the carpet to the tackstrip (Fig. 7-31). The carpet is now stretched in. Finish the job by trimming around the perimeter, then tuck the edge of the carpet into the gully between the tackstrip and the wall.

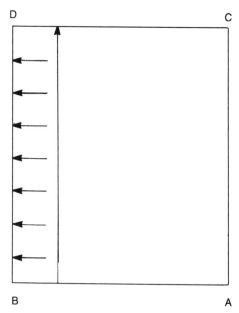

Fig. 7-28. Installing Axminster weave carpet. Step two. Power stretch from corner B to corner D and hook the carpet. Use straight knee kicks along wall B–D and hook the carpet.

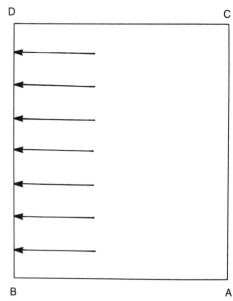

Fig. 7-29. Installing Axminster weave carpet. Step three. Power stretch along wall A–C and hook the carpet along wall B–D.

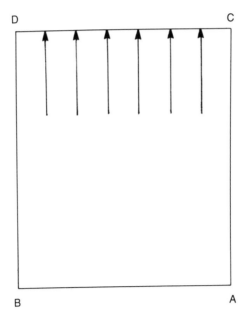

Fig. 7-30. Installing Axminster weave carpet. Step four. Power stretch along wall B–A and hook the carpet along wall D–C.

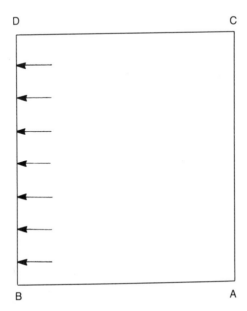

Fig. 7-31. Installing Axminster weave carpet. Step five. Use straight knee kicks and hook the carpet along wall B–D.

Tufted Carpet Installation

Seaming and stretching tufted carpet is less tedious. Cut edges do not ravel as easily as woven fabrics, so seam sealing is only necessary along cut edges to be seamed, not along walls. Loop-pile carpet, however, must be sealed along all edges. A strip of seaming tape is placed evenly under the two pieces to be joined. This tape has up to nine parallel rows of hardened glue set on heavy, puckered paper (Fig. 7-32). A special seaming iron with a wide, flat bottom is heated electrically to melt the glue and spread it as the iron is moved along the length of the tape (Figs. 7-33, 7-34).

Every foot or so you should pause in order to fold the edges of the fabric down into the hot glue, pressing the edges together

Fig. 7-32. A roll of seaming tape.

Fig. 7-33. The seaming iron melts the glue on the seaming tape.

to form a closely butted seam and allowing the glue to set up and harden (Fig. 7-35). Care must be taken not to overlap any portion of the seam. Overlaps make the pile higher on one side of the seam than the other, thus making a seam that is highly visible. The face yarns must also be prevented from getting into the glue and sticking there.

Be sure not to move the iron along too quickly as this does not allow the glue to spread evenly and makes a seam that peaks or does not lie flat. Once the glue cools, the two pieces of carpet are fused into one strong sheet of material. A seam tractor is sometimes used to blend in seams.

Hot-seaming of tufted carpet is fast and effective. Well-made seams are hardly noticeable (do not expect completely invisible seams

Fig. 7-34. The flat bottom of the seaming iron.

especially with short nap carpeting) and withstand repeated cleanings. Popular myths notwithstanding, seamed areas wear as well as unseamed areas as long as the glue sticks to the backing and the seam tape does not break.

After seaming, the carpet is stretched into place. Tufted carpet stretches in all directions and, like the other constructions, are installed in a predetermined sequence. Here is the proper way to stretch in tufted carpet.

Begin by hooking the carpet onto the tackstrip pins at corner A (Fig. 7-36). Put the block of the power stretcher at corner A, then power stretch from A to C and hook the carpet onto the tackstrip at corner C. Next, put the block of the power stretcher at corner A and power stretch from A to B and hook the carpet onto the tackstrip at corner B (Fig. 7-37).

Then use the knee kicker and bump at a 15-degree angle to hook the carpet onto the tackstrip along the entire wall A-C (Fig. 7-38). Do the same thing along the wall A-B. Knee kick every few feet at a 15-degree angle and hook the carpet onto the tackstrip (Fig. 7-39).

Fig. 7-35. Working the back of the carpet into the melted glue.

Fig. 7-36. Installing tufted carpet. Step one. Power stretch from corner A to corner C and hook the carpet.

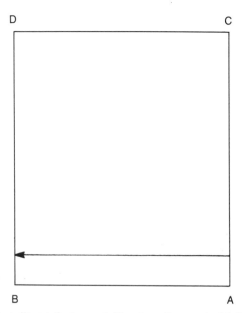

Fig. 7-37. Installing tufted carpet. Step two. Power stretch from corner A to corner B and hook the carpet.

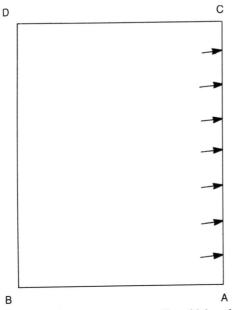

Fig. 7-38. Installing tufted carpet. Step three. Knee kick and hook along wall A to C.

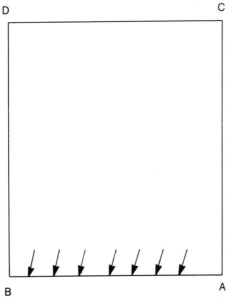

Fig. 7-39. Installing tufted carpet. Step four. Knee kick at a 15-degree angle and hook along wall A–B.

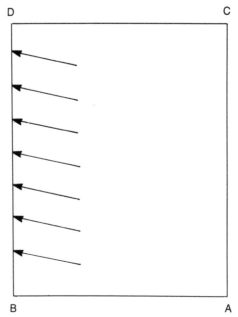

Fig. 7-40. Installing tufted carpet. Step five. Power stretch at a 15-degree angle and hook along wall B–D.

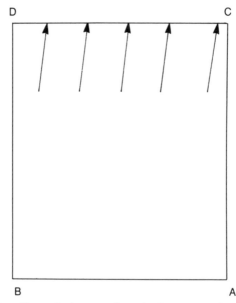

Fig. 7-41. Installing tufted carpet. Step six. Power stretch at a 15-degree angle and hook along wall D–C.

Next, put the stretcher block in corner A and power stretch at a 15-degree angle, moving the stretcher every few feet along wall B-D and hook the carpet onto the tackstrip from B to D (Fig. 7-40). Finally, put the stretcher head in corner B and power stretch along the wall D-C and hook the carpet in the same manner along the wall (Fig. 7-41). Trim the excess carpet with the edge trimmer and push the edge of the carpet into the gully between the tackstrip and wall with the stair tool or a wide blade to finish the job.

Properly installed carpet should be smooth around the edges and tight in the center of the room. Some people like to use an electric staple gun to fasten the carpet to the tackstrip. This practice not only makes "dimples" around the edge of a room, it leaves a loose installation because the fabric is stapled to the edges instead of being stretched in.

Installing Glue-down Carpet

Glue-down jute, synthetic-backed, and woven carpet are installed in a different manner. The carpet selvedges are trimmed, seam sealer is applied, and the drop and fill pieces are ready for seaming. Then the carpet is pulled up to halfway back down the room and a special adhesive is applied directly to the smooth, clean floor, whether concrete, plywood, tile, linoleum, or hardwood.

A notched trowel is used to spread the glue. The depth of the notch determines how thick a layer of glue is spread. This in turn is determined by the roughness of the carpet backing. The more uneven and corrugated the backing (as with Axminster) the more glue is needed.

The carpet is rolled out onto the glue and against the walls. The fabric is trimmed and seam sealer is applied to all cut edges, whether woven or tufted carpet. A roller weighing up to 40 pounds is used to remove any air pockets and ensure that the carpet sticks well. Everything must remain off the carpet for at least 24 hours. A special type of glue, known as quick release cement, is used when a good bond is needed but the carpet must be removed at a future time. This type of adhesive allows the fabric to be easily pulled up from the floor without leaving a sticky mess or shredded fabric.

Rubber-backed or foam-backed carpets are cut, fit, and glued down in a manner similar to jute-backed. Use just enough glue to ensure a good bond. Too much glue can wick up into the foam back and cause it to become hard and collapse. *It is extremely important to apply seam sealer to all cut edges in order to avoid ravelling,* especially with looped-pile carpet (Fig. 7-42).

So many otherwise competent installers leave out the seam sealer, thinking that the floor glue will hold the tufts in place. The seam sealer welds the two sheets of fabric together into one strong unit. It prevents ragged tufts from getting caught in the vacuum beater bar and pulling out. Just one or two rows need to pull out before the rubber backing begins to separate from the primary back with pile yarns in it. Then the whole seam begins to let go. This whole problem is so easy to prevent!

PROFESSIONAL INSTALLATION

Now that you know all about installing your own carpet, a word to the wise is needed here. All first-quality carpet comes with a 1-

Fig. 7-42. Carpet that has unravelled along an unlatexed edge.

year unconditional warranty covering defects in manufacturing and workmanship. However, many, if not most, mills will not cover carpet that is installed by a do-it-yourselfer. Professionals are warned not to install carpet that has a defect, obvious or not, because the mills do not like to take back carpet that has been cut. This feeling is extended to the self-installer because most amateurs are not familiar enough with carpet to recognize a defect if they see one. So, do-it-yourself installers, beware! You could get stuck with a lot of carpet if a problem develops.

If you are discouraged from installing your own carpet, take heart. You do have other choices. You can hire a freelance installer, or you can use the workroom offered by the carpet shop or designer.

Hiring an independent installer has its pros and cons. By checking references, you can find qualified crews. Independents often cost less than unionized workroom labor, and their work can be of the highest standards. Jobs are personalized and customized. However, many independents work on a shoestring and can ill afford any problems. If a complaint regarding workmanship or materials should arise, some freelancers would be hard pressed to handle the problem. They just could not afford the delay to their cash flow.

Virtually all carpet shops and decorators offer in-house carpet installation as part of their "total package" philosophy. Most people assume that a dealer's installers will do a top-notch job. That is not necessarily the case. Larger stores keep several crews busy and, unfortunately, quality can vary from crew to crew.

It is best, once again, to check references and quality of work. Ideally, you should be able to see finished installations in order to check the workmanship. It is a shame to spend a lot of money on a beautiful carpet, only to have it ruined by a poor installation.

As a rule, in-house installers are very good. The dealer could not afford to keep a bad installer around for a long time. Although installation is the installer's responsibility, both the dealer and the consumer have a large stake in how well the job is done.

Whichever alternative you decide to pursue, once the carpet is installed and furniture is placed in the room, you will enjoy it more because you understand about both the carpet and the installation.

8

Carpet Maintenance

What can you do to keep your beautiful and expensive carpeting looking like new? Plan to care for your carpet in a number of ways involving both short- and long-term maintenance. In the short term, regular vacuuming and spotting works wonders to keep the carpet looking good. Over the long term, plan on professional cleaning to maintain your investment.

VACUUM CLEANERS

Regular vacuuming is probably the single most helpful thing a person can do to maintain a carpet's appearance. How often to vacuum depends on traffic and lifestyle. It is suggested that under average household conditions (four people, one pet), a carpet should be vacuumed at least twice a week—once lightly, once thoroughly. A light vacuuming consists of two to three forward and back passes of the machine in each of the high usage areas, with one pass in the low usage areas.

Heavy vacuuming means at least six back and forth passes of the machine in the high traffic areas, one to two in the other areas. It is a lot of work, but your carpet will thank you for it by staying new-looking longer and your pocketbook will thank you because the carpet will need less frequent cleanings. Remember that grit and sand rubbing at the base of the fibers is what causes a carpet to get dull and worn looking.

Can a carpet be vacuumed too much? Today's synthetic fabrics are made to be vacuumed. Many maintain their appearance only by vacuuming. Normally, most machines work well with most kinds of fabrics, but heavy-duty machines teamed with delicate fabrics such as wool or some acrylics can cause problems. Strong motors and stiff brushes can distort cut-pile patterns and make berber-type looped fabrics shed heavily and look stringy. It is better to set the brushes up so they barely touch the pile rather than beat the carpet to death.

When looking for a vacuum, how do you make a good selection? As with many other things in this world, information provided by the manufacturer or a salesperson can be confusing at best. In general, according to tests performed by the independent Carpet and Rug Institute, upright vacuums (Fig. 8-1) consistently outperform

Fig. 8-1. An upright vacuum cleaner.

tank-type or canisters (Fig. 8-2), even when the tanks have a separate power-driven beater-bar attachment known as a power head (Fig. 8-3). And yet, many vacuum salespeople insist that tank-type machines with add-on power heads are more powerful and efficient than uprights.

Fig. 8-2. A tank-type or canister vacuum with a suction-only (non-beater bar) nozzle.

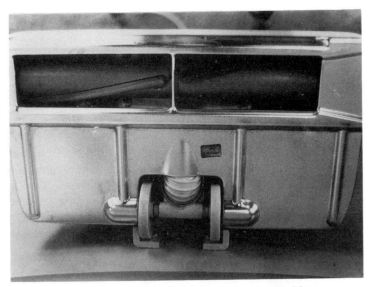

Fig. 8-3. A canister power head with beater brushes and bars.

The fact is that an upright agitates the pile yarns better and creates a more efficient partial vacuum inside the suction chamber. Uprights which fill from the top are the most efficient and blow less dust around than bottom-filling models. Of course, a machine must be used to be effective. It can't work if it just sits in a closet!

Vacuum maintenance is also very important. Any machine needs to be looked at occasionally, and a vacuum cleaner is no exception. A weak vacuum cannot pick up dirt and lint. A clean vacuum bag does wonders to increase suction and efficiency. A full bag is probably the most common reason that a machine works improperly. Bags fill up more quickly than many people realize, so keep an eye on them.

Worn out beater bar brushes do not provide the correct agitation to loosen soil from the yarn and lift it from the carpet backing. Look at the brushes occasionally and see if they are frayed or worn down. Often string or pet hair will wrap around the brushes and keep them from working properly. Cut away any foreign material and keep the brushes clean. If the brushes look stubbly, replace them with new ones. Remember, the brushes must touch the carpet at least slightly in order to remove the dirt.

Check the belt now and then. Replace it if it looks cracked or weak. A broken belt not only creates an inconvenience, but the hot rubber from a broken belt will put a black streak on the carpet which may not come out.

SPOT REMOVERS

Everyone gets a spot on their carpet occasionally, and many remedies, both store-bought and homemade, are available. Choosing the right spotter depends on the type of spill. Most spills in the home are divided into two main groups—water-based and oil-based. Water-based spills include milk, juices, and carbonated beverages. Oil-based spots are cooking oils, butter, car oil, and tar, to name a few.

By and large, the aerosol spotters available in grocery stores help less than most people would expect. The problem with most spray-foam carpet cleaners is inherent to their cleaning properties—the soapy foam. This goop is supposed to remove all types of spots, but most of the time it only buries the spot under a layer of suds. Optical brighteners in the foam make it appear that the spot is gone. Adding insult to injury, the foam soon begins to attract dirt because of the foam's stickiness, and the spot slowly reappears.

Rinsing would normally reduce or eliminate the resoiling problem, but the foam is devilishly difficult to remove, even by a professional. To make matters worse, some of these cleaners can slowly bleach the color out of the fabric. Spot testing first is not always a help because the lightning occurs so slowly that it may not be noticeable for days or even weeks. If the color is not actually bleached, the optical brighteners literally cover up the carpet dye and leave a light area. These brighteners attach themselves permanently to the carpet fibers and cannot be removed.

PROPER SPOT CLEANING

So what is a person to do? Fortunately, everyone has the compound needed to remove at least water-based spots—water! That's right, plain water removes these spots. The challenge is to remove the foreign matter, usually sugar, without fuzzing or distorting the face yarns. (Shorter nap carpets are, of course, easier to work with than longer naps.)

Blot up the excess spill with a terry cloth towel, then apply more water with a trigger-type spray bottle after the first blotting. How much depends on the size of the spot and the thickness of the carpet. Do not soak the fabric, and try to work from the outside in to keep the spot from getting bigger. *Do not rub.*

Apply enough so that the sugars can dissolve. Blot again and feel the fabric. If it doesn't feel clean, repeat the above steps several times. Remember: blot, don't rub. Rubbing will untwist the yarn and make the pile look fuzzy when it dries.

If the spill contains a color as well as sugar, little can be done to remove the color. Natural colors such as red wine or blue grape juice will most often stain a carpet permanently, especially once the spot dries. Artificial colors such as those found in Kool-Aid and even many types of soda pop will stain. Sometimes putting white wine onto red wine will remove the stain. Club soda often removes stains containing artificial colors if put on immediately.

Once dried, a water-based spot must be rewet in order to begin dissolving the sugars. This is best done using a plastic pump or trigger-type hand sprayer and a soft-bristled brush on a handle, such as a dishwashing brush. Spray the spot until just moistened and brush gently in one direction only, being careful not to distort the yarns. Work in the water and loosen any particles.

It may be necessary to add a few drops of liquid dish detergent to the water to promote removal of foreign particles (such as orange rind or mud). If any detergents are used, it is most important to rinse the fabric thoroughly with clear water once the spot is removed. Otherwise, the soap residue will attract soil and the spot will reappear. Blot up, using terry cloth towels and rewet as needed. Once the affected area feels clean and not soapy slick, the spot is gone and should not return.

Oily stains are removed with solvents that dissolve the foreign substance from the yarn. Common preparations purchased in the household section of most stores include Energine, Thuro, and Goddard's dry-cleaning fluids. Apply a few drops to the spot, brush gently in one direction, and blot. A second application may be necessary to remove any traces from the fabric.

Dry-cleaning fluid evaporates without a ring and does not need rinsing. It also removes tar, grease, and small amounts of candlewax safely. Use it sparingly; too much can eat away the latex bond between the two backings, causing the yarn to fall out.

Avoid using gasoline, kerosene, paint removers, or other highly flammable or otherwise strong solvents. Call a professional if household remedies do not help. It is better to spend a little money than ruin a fine carpet or risk your health or life just to try and remove a spot.

ODORS

Invisible odors are as much an annoyance as stains. Carpet fresheners and deodorizers do not help much, no matter how much is spent by their manufacturers to tout them. Most odors are caused by microorganisms living somewhere in the carpet, and dumping perfumed baking soda on them doesn't do anything to remove them from the carpet. Their "food" can be milk, urine, water, or any number of substances which support bacterial growth.

Deodorizers which are sprayed or sprinkled simply cover up the odors but do not attack the source. The foreign substance must be removed in order to get rid of the odor-causing bacteria. Sometimes, as with severe mildew or saturation by urine, replacement of the carpet and pad is the only sure cure. On occasion, pets will soak a favorite area of carpet so that the underlying floor is also affected. Then the carpet must be taken up, the pad replaced, and the floor refinished and sealed to keep any remaining odor locked in.

Packaged fresheners cannot cure these problems. The best solution is to keep up with spots and have the carpet cleaned on a regular basis. A competent professional has chemicals in his arsenal which completely neutralize (as opposed to masking) the offending odor. A good cleaner knows how to inject the chemical into the pad if necessary. Of course, prevention is the best medicine.

DO-IT-YOURSELF CLEANING

Many people like to do-it-themselves when it comes to cleaning carpets, even though the methods are physically demanding and the results are not always as good as one might hope. It is easy to rent a variety of cleaning equipment similar to what a professional would use. Let's look at the three most popular methods used, including shampooing, dry cleaning, and steam cleaning.

Shampooing

Rotary shampooing is the oldest method for cleaning carpets. It is what most people think of when the phrase "carpet cleaning" is mentioned. A shampoo machine uses one or two flat, rotating brushes to work a shampoo solution into the pile yarns. The mechanical action of the brushes combines with the shampoo to lift the dirt from the yarn and break any oil film. After the carpet dries, the shampoo turns to a powder which is vacuumed up along with any remaining soil.

While shampooing leaves the carpet looking clean, most of the dirt has in fact been driven to the carpet backing and covered with a layer of detergent film. Because there is no way to rinse and extract the shampoo and dirt, it all remains in the carpet pile. This residue leads to a rapid resoiling and the argument that because a carpet gets dirty so quickly after cleaning, it must be better to wait as long as possible to clean it the first time. That is why most people either use a wet vac to remove as much solution as possible or, better yet, rinse and extract the fabric using a steam cleaner. A combination of shampoo and extraction is the best method for cleaning heavily soiled carpeting.

Shampooing has two more risks associated with it. It is easy to overwet the carpet causing shrinking or delamination (the secondary backing comes off). Also, the scrubbing action of the brushes can distort some cut-pile fabrics, untwisting the face yarns and making the carpet look fuzzy. Non-wool loop fabrics withstand shampooing better.

Dry Cleaning

Dry cleaning involves an absorbent powder impregnated with a volatile cleaning solvent that is sprinkled onto the carpet pile, and a machine with opposing rotary brushes that work the powder into the yarns (Fig. 8-4). The solvent evaporates and frees soil trapped in the yarn, which is absorbed by the powder. The powder and soil are then vacuumed up. In high traffic areas with a lot of soil, a traffic lane cleaner is often sprayed on before the powder is applied. This chemical helps loosen soil and dissolve spots and increases overall cleaning power.

Dry cleaning has its good points. The carpet can be walked on right away because it is not wet. The equipment is easy to use, and it is impossible to overwet the fabric. Dry cleaning is also good for touching up high-traffic areas between professional cleanings and leaves very little residue behind when done correctly. It works best on light to moderately soiled fabrics which are not heavily spotted.

The dry method also has a few disadvantages to consider. The brushes can cause tip flair and distortion on some high-profile, cut-pile fabrics. The powder is difficult to remove from longer naps, and can build up into a residue after several cleanings, causing a resoiling factor.

"Steam" Cleaning

"Steam cleaning" is a misleading name for the most effective cleaning method. Actually, no steam is used at all. A hot water/cleaning agent mixture is sprayed under pressure into the face yarns, dissolving soil from the yarns and lifting the dirt into a suspension (Fig. 8-5). A vacuum behind the pressure jets removes water and soil almost immediately, leaving a damp fabric. The dirty water goes

Fig. 8-4. The Host dry carpet cleaning machine.

into a holding tank built into the machine. (Hot water extraction is a longer but more accurate name for this system.)

Hot-water extraction has several advantages over the other cleaning methods. It removes more soil and more types of soil than shampooing or dry powder. Because it uses no brushes, there is virtually no chance for pile distortion. Residue buildup and consequent

Fig. 8-5. A small portable hot-water extraction carpet cleaner.

resoiling is kept to a minimum. The system has one big disadvantage for the novice. Repeated cleaning of a heavily soiled area can cause overwetting, with resulting damage (mildew, delamination, subfloor warping, etc.).

Keep in mind that the chemicals used with rental machines are often watered down to make them ''goof-proof.'' That means heavily soiled areas are more difficult to clean completely than if professional strength chemicals were used. Repeatedly cleaning a problem area will not result in a markedly cleaner carpet, only a wetter one. If a dirty area doesn't come clean after two or three tries, give up. Do-it-yourself carpet cleaning is one of the more difficult tasks in the home, and the results do not come close to a thorough professional cleaning.

PROFESSIONAL CLEANING

So, when *should* you consider professional cleaning? It is true that professional anything costs more than doing it yourself. But most of the time you get a good return for your investment.

A professional cleaner should have chemicals and equipment which are not available to the average consumer, not to mention a wealth of experience to deal with most any problem relating to a soiled carpet. And the results are normally a lot more satisfying. Sure, there are a lot of horror stories about this cleaner who soaked a carpet so badly that it was wet for three days, or that cleaner who left so much residue in the carpet that it was dirty again three weeks later. But most carpet cleaners are at least competent, and some are truly excellent at their craft. Using a professional cleaner on your expensive carpeting is a wise choice.

Take a long look at your carpet when considering cleaning. Check the color. Does it look faded or grayish? Look at the face pile. Are the tufts stuck together? Is soil visible? Is the nap badly crushed? Professional cleaning should alleviate all these problems and also remove most all common spots.

Most experts recommend cleaning carpets every 12 to 18 months for longest life. Light colors or high-traffic areas could need cleaning more often. You should not wait until the traffic areas are so dirty that they look like a path in the woods. Soil and spots are harder to remove once they've been in a fabric a long time. And spots that would have come out when fairly fresh-set are sometimes impossible to remove after months pass. So keep your carpet cleaner busy and keep your carpet looking nice.

Locating a Professional Cleaner

If you need a good cleaner, you must find one the same way you would if you were looking for a good interior designer or carpet layer. Ask everyone you know about their carpet cleaning experiences and who they recommend. Call a couple of the larger retail carpet stores and ask for recommendations. Sooner or later a few names will dominate your list. These names are your best bet.

Pick one of the names on the list and call for further information. Ask a lot of questions. Make it sound like you really know the cleaning business.

○ What method of cleaning is used? (Almost any type of properly running truck-mounted hot-water extraction system is generally acknowledged to be the best all-around system.)

○ How much experience do the workers have? (It's nice to provide jobs and help the economy grow, but why should someone learn on *your* carpet?)

○ What type of cleaning agents are used? (Generally, soapless detergents and emulsifiers are best for general soil. Special spotters are needed for grease, rust, blood, and chewing gum.)

○ Is prespotting included in the regular cleaning price? (It usually is.)

○ How are stairs figured? (Sometimes per stair, sometimes per square foot.)

○ What about furniture? (Most places figure furniture moving in the overall price. A few give discounts for empty rooms.)

If the person answering your questions is confident and sounds intelligent, rejoice. You might have found your cleaner.

Then ask the *big* question: *How much do you charge?* Most really good carpet cleaners fall into a fairly narrow price range—from moderately expensive to expensive. The most expensive in town won't necessarily do a better job than someone charging a little less, but expect to spend some money. You do get what you pay for. After checking with a few places on your list, you'll get a good idea of an average price. Most carpet cleaners charge by the square foot, not by room. If the total price seems reasonable and you are pleased by the recommendations of others, make an appointment and get the carpet cleaned.

It should go without saying that if something seems too good to be true, it probably is. The story of the consumer who saw a flyer advertising any room steam-cleaned for $4.95 (minimum three rooms) is typical. "What a deal," thought the consumer. "I can get the living room, family room, and dining room cleaned for less than 15 bucks." So an appointment was made, and a technician came out to clean the carpet. The machine was loud and not much bigger than the one for rent in the supermarket, and it took a long time to clean the three rooms.

After the work was finished, the consumer was handed a bill—for $89.85! "Why is the bill so high?", demanded the consumer. "What happened to the $14.85?" The technician calmly explained, "The steam cleaning was $14.85, all right. But the carpet was so dirty that I had to use a special conditioner which is $25 per gallon, and I had to use one gallon in each room. That makes the total $89.85."

After a lot of argument, the consumer finally paid the bill, knowing it wouldn't happen again. The moral of the story is very simple: don't jump at bargain carpet cleaning without checking it out.

Professional Cleaning Methods

Four types of cleaning methods are available to the professionals: shampoo, dry foam, dry powder, and steam cleaning (hot water extraction).

Shampoo. With the shampoo method, a cleaning solution is dispensed from a tank to the cleaning brush, which is around 15 inches in diameter (Fig. 8-6). The brush scrubs the solution into the carpet pile, where the shampoo lifts the dirt off the face yarn and holds it in suspension. The most satisfactory long-term results are achieved when shampooing is used together with a rinse-and-extract system to flush out the soil and shampoo residue. Shampooing is often used when the carpet is too dirty for cleaning with hot water extraction alone. The operator must take care not to overwet the carpet or allow cut-pile fabrics to fuzz.

Dry Foam. The dry-foam system uses rotating brushes to apply a drier type of shampoo to the carpet pile, along with a wet vacuum pickup to remove water and dirt. Because less water is used, the carpet dries more quickly. It leaves less of a residue than ordinary shampooing, and fuzzing is reduced with cut-pile fabrics. The carpet should be rinsed and extracted with this method for best long-term results.

Dry Clean. Dry-powder cleaning has been around a long time, and while marketing strategies would have us believe otherwise, the basic way the system works hasn't changed much. A powder—either chemical or natural—is brushed or otherwise worked into the carpet face yarns, where they absorb grit and oils. Main walkways are first treated with a traffic lane cleaner to loosen any heavy soil.

After a short time, the powder and, hopefully, most of the dirt sticking to it is vacuumed up and the carpet is ready for immediate

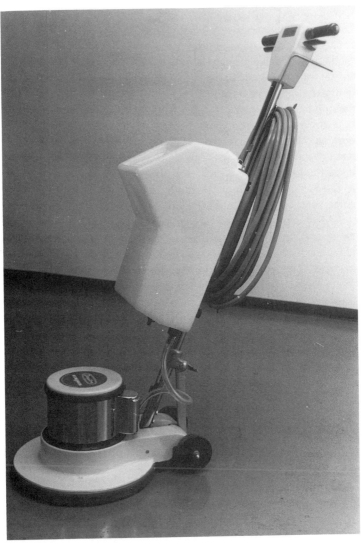

Fig. 8-6. A carpet shampooer.

use. Dry cleaning leaves little residue if the powder is completely removed. It works best on lightly soiled fabrics as a between steam cleanings method. It is the least inconvenient method in terms of consumer discomfort or inconvenience.

Hot-Water Extraction. Steam cleaning, or hot-water extraction, is probably the best overall system used by professionals today. There are two types of equipment used: portable and truckmounted. Portable equipment is moveable on wheels. The better portable machines are many times more powerful than most rental units, and some approach the power of the smaller truck mounts. A portable machine is easy to carry on and off the job, easy to set up and easy to handle. They are especially suited for commercial jobs several stories up, or a long distance from the parking lot where truckmounts could not reach.

However, a truck-mounted hot water extraction system—from here on called a steam cleaner for simplicity—is much more powerful and is especially useful for residential cleaning. The operator pulls up to the front door, unwinds the hoses for hot water and vacuum to the farthest point to be cleaned, attaches the hoses to the machine in the back of the van, and is ready to begin cleaning.

Most consumers find truck-mounted steam cleaning preferable for several reasons. The machine stays outside and there is no chance of bumping into furniture or knocking something over with a heavy machine. The truckmounts have thermostats to control the water temperature so that each type of carpet such as wool or nylon is properly treated. The water comes out at a very high pressure (around 400-500 pounds per square inch) so that very little water is needed to wash or rinse the fabric.

In fact, the vacuum is so strong that over 90 percent of the water (and the dirt in it) is removed during cleaning. As a result, carpets dry relatively quickly and spots do not tend to come back. Most of these machines can be set so that the cleaning solution is shut off and a hot water rinse is used after cleaning. This very important final rinse removes all the cleaner as well as any remaining soil. The carpet literally feels squeaky clean with no slick soap feel.

The carpet will stay clean just as long as when it was new. There is no residue in the yarn to cause rapid resoiling. When carpets are cleaned this way, the old wives' tale about carpets getting dirtier right after cleaning is finally laid to rest. In fact, side by side cleanings comparing truck mounts to other systems always show the truck mounts coming out on top.

But *knowing* about home cleaning methods and professional cleaning systems is only one part of the solution to keep your carpets looking good. *Doing* something with that knowledge is the other half to the equation. Remember the 12- to 18-month rule of thumb for regular cleaning: more with light colors and/or high-traffic areas, less with dark colors and/or little-used rooms.

Today's synthetic fabrics rarely wear out from too much use. They instead slowly ''fade'' away under layers of dirt and shampoo.

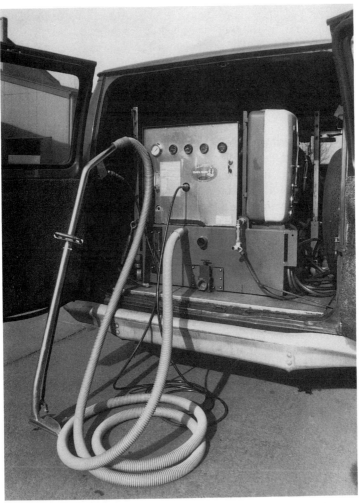

Fig. 8-7. A truck-mounted hot-water extraction carpet cleaning machine.

Take care of your floor coverings and they will last so long you will
get tired of the color long before the fabric needs replacing because
of wear.

CARPET PROTECTORS

What kind of protection should you give your carpeting after it
is cleaned? Because it is obvious that proper cleaning does not take
the life out of a carpet, is there anything that you can do to keep
the carpet looking good until the next cleaning?

The "advanced generation" nylons—Anso IV made by Allied and Antron III by Du Pont—have built-in soil protection which never wears or cleans off. The protection lasts as long as the carpet fiber. There is no need to spray on any topical applications.

But what should you do if your carpet has "generic" nylon, or if it's polyester or acrylic? Perhaps you don't know if the carpet came with Scotchgard or whether protectant was put on before you bought the house?

Scotchgard is a fabric protector made by 3 M Company. It is widely known and used on all fabrics from wearing apparel to wall and upholstery fabrics to carpeting. Teflon is a similar protector made by Du Pont. Both of them use a fluorocarbon to bond onto the yarn fibers. The chemicals are sprayed onto the carpet either in the mill after the carpet is completely finished, or in your home after the carpet is cleaned.

Once on the fabric, the soil protection is very difficult to remove. This means that the protection goes through several cleanings before all of it is gone. It is estimated that Scotchgard and Teflon lose around 20 percent of their soil-retarding quality with each cleaning. It is not necessary to put on fresh protector after each cleaning. Enough remains so that reapplication is needed after perhaps three or four cleanings. In fact, it is possible to make a carpet stiff by applying too much soil retardant.

Cleaners like to put it on after each cleaning because it is a good "add on" item. One word of caution: only put these protectors on a very clean carpet. They will seal in any dirt left on the carpet fibers and make it almost impossible to remove that soil the next time the carpet is cleaned.

The second type of soil retardants contain a silicone base. Fiberseal is a well-known brand. The silicone-based protectors work the same way repelling soil as the fluorocarbon protectors, and last through about as many cleanings.

Either of these two types of protectors work well on polyester and acrylic carpets, as well as the generic nylons. They will wear off eventually if subjected to a lot of traffic, but in normal home use last a long time. If you are not sure if your carpet has any protection, try the bead test to find out. The different protectors make liquids bead up on the surface so that they can be cleaned up easily before the spill has a chance to soak into the fabric.

Take a small amount of water and pour it on the carpet. If the water beads up, the carpet is probably protected. If it soaks in right away, you might want to consider having a protector put on after the next cleaning. But remember: it doesn't do any good to put a soil protector on a carpet full of cleaning residue. The protector will seal in the residue and the carpet will look dull when it dries. Make sure the carpet is completely rinsed before any soil retardants are applied.

Do not expect too much from topically applied or inherent protectors. They do keep dirt from sticking as easily to carpet yarn, make it easier to remove spills, and allow the carpet to clean more easily. But certain substances stain and bleach fibers whether they are protected or not. There is nothing available that will protect against all substances. And even protected yarns get dirty and need cleaning occasionally. Soil does collect even in the advanced generation yarns and must be removed on a regular basis.

9

Common Characteristics and Defects

So often, a consumer makes a major purchase, such as carpeting, only to be surprised by the product's performance. This section explains normal characteristics and typical defects that are common to all carpet in all price ranges. Some things that are considered normal by the carpet industry appear as defects to the untrained eye. Many misunderstandings could be avoided if more people understood exactly what to expect from new carpet. Unfortunately, these things are hardly ever brought up during the selling of the carpet.

SHEDDING

Shedding is common to all new carpet, especially cut-pile carpet, whether made from continuous filament or staple yarns. Some fuzz is produced by the shearing process and remains in the pile, and the consumer must vacuum out the fluff. It takes anywhere from 2 weeks to 3 months to remove most of the fuzz, and it may appear that large amounts of yarn are disappearing into the vacuum bag.

One advantage of carpet made with continuous filament yarn is that once the initial fuzz is gone, the fabric stops shedding entirely. With the more common staple yarns, the carpet always sheds at least a little. Certain short staple-spun yarns used in plush fabrics shed abundantly throughout the life of the carpet. Sometimes shedding is not normal. If all of the filaments which are spun together to form a tuft are not securely locked into the primary backing by the latex glue, filament slippage results with excess fuzzing and pilling. Contact your carpet dealer if you feel the shedding is excessive.

PILLING

Pilling is a condition directly related to shedding. If the vacuum cleaner cannot keep up with the amount of fluff coming from the pile, the fluff collects on the surface of the carpet. From walking and scuffing of shoes (especially sneakers), the fuzz rolls up into little balls called pills. Soon the carpet looks like an old sweater.

Pilling is usually normal, especially with acrylics and wool pile. It also happens with nylon carpet. If objectionable, the pills can be sheared by hand using a sheep shearer Your store can send out a professional to do the job. The condition usually affects new carpet only and does not return once the fabric is sheared.

SHADING

Shading and pile reversal are common complaints among people who have cut-pile carpeting in their homes. *Shading* is an apparent color difference between areas of the same carpet. It ranges in intensity from slight to severe and is caused by face yarns which have changed the direction of their lay. Footprints and marks from the wheels of the vacuum are one type of shading, caused by the face yarns crushing down. (People have been known to be so upset by their carpet—especially the thicker, longer naps—showing footprints that they have ripped up new carpet, thrown it out, and replaced it with something that won't show marks.)

When the face yarns change direction, light is reflected from the yarn sides and yarn tips at different rates, making light and dark areas. Shading is normal for all cut-pile fabrics because the pile does not always lie in one direction. Because it is a characteristic of a certain type of fabric, mills rarely consider shading a legitimate complaint.

Shading does not occur in all cut-pile fabrics, and it is impossible to predict which ones will shade, reverse, or watermark. If a cut-pile carpet is chosen (and it *is* the most popular style today), some degree of shading is likely.

Fig. 9-1. Carpet pile that exhibits pooling or watermarking.

PILE REVERSAL

While shading is seen all over cut-pile fabrics, *pile reversal* is most noticeable in high-traffic areas and pivot points, such as doorways or around corners. The pile yarns tend to lay on their sides in these areas and look darker than the rest of the carpet. This is equivalent to crushed velvet furniture fabrics, with their light and dark shades.

Some people think shading and pile reversal are ugly because the color is uneven. Others consider it the mark of a fine-quality carpet. At any rate, mills will not replace a carpet that shows pile reversal because they know that the replacement will reverse, too.

Pooling

Pooling or *watermarking* is the most severe form of pile reversal (Fig. 9-1). The face yarns reverse direction and sometimes lie almost flat in an irregular circle which can reach several feet across. The areas look dark, as if someone had poured a bucket of water onto the carpet, hence the name "watermark." It is not possible to permanently correct any shading, since the face yarns can always change direction.

Roll Crush

One type of pile reversal, found only in new carpet, is called *roll crush* or *roll crush marks*. This occurs most often when a large roll of carpet develops a flat spot when the roll loosens. The carpet pile in the flat areas is crushed and its direction is reversed. When the carpet is unrolled, a series of widthwise bands or streaks run down the length of the roll (Fig. 9-2). Roll crush marks are usually 2 to 4 feet apart. The distance between them depends on the distance from the center of the roll. Inner-roll crush marks are 1 to 2 feet apart, those farther away from the core might be 3 to 5 feet apart. The appearance varies widely, however, from a crease to overall distortion and a wrinkled appearance.

Unlike other forms of pile reversal, roll crush sometimes goes away by itself just from vacuuming and walking, especially if the condition is slight. Because of high humidity and yarn blossom, the yarns frequently correct their direction after a few weeks. If the condition persists, the marks can be easily and permanently removed. Just as ironing a shirt with a steam iron removes wrinkles, applying steam to the carpet pile relaxes the fibers. When steamed and gently brushed (Fig. 9-3), the pile returns to its normal direction and the streaks disappear. Your dealer can send a professional to steam the carpet in your home.

Ideally, a dry steam should be used, from a machine like a Jiffy Steamer (Fig. 9-4) or a similar type. Such machines boil water in a self-contained tank and the resulting steam goes through a plastic hose and out through a flat nozzle with several holes. These steamers are also used to remove wrinkles from clothing and draperies and are very safe for all fabrics. Because the carpet remains dry, it can

Fig. 9-2. Carpet pile with roll crush marks.

Fig. 9-3. Hand steaming the pile to remove a roll crush mark.

Fig. 9-4. A Jiffy Steamer is used to remove crush marks, pile reversal, and creases from carpet pile.

be used almost immediately after service. If dry steamers are not available, steam cleaning with very hot water and no cleaning solution should do the trick. (Note: Acrylic, polyester, and olefin carpets do not accept moisture and will not respond to any steam treatments to correct roll crushing.)

CRUSHING/MATTING

Crushing and matting are two common problems that people often confuse. Any carpet will crush somewhat underfoot, whether looped-pile or cut-pile. Longer piles tend to crush more than shorter naps. Footprints and traffic lanes result from crushing. Crushing is normal. *Matting* occurs when the tips of cut-pile yarns untwist and fray, and get tangled in the neighboring tufts. If the tufts untwist ⅓ of their length or more, and if the affected area is all over and not in a confined area subject to unusual usage, the carpet is generally considered defective if not more than a year old.

Matting and untwisting happen when the heat-set of the yarn is weak. This condition is similar to a bad permanent wave that does not hold its set and allows the curl to relax. A poorly heat-set yarn looses its resiliency and untwists, packing down the fabric and making it look flat and worn. Matting is not common today.

BLEEDING/CROCKING

Bleeding and crocking are two problems that refer to degree of dye fastness. *Bleeding* occurs when the carpet gets wet, either by cleaning or flooding, and the color runs. It is most common with darker shades, especially reds and blues, because large amounts of dye are used in order to achieve the rich colors. Even when rinsed thoroughly by the mill, some dye residues often remain. Don't panic if the cleaning solution picks up some color the first time your red carpet is cleaned. If the condition seems excessive, tests by the mill can determine the level of dye fastness.

Crocking means color rub-off. It can happen whether the fabric is wet or dry. Characteristically, light-colored shoes or clothes begin to turn the same color as the carpet. Sometimes the condition is corrected by cleaning the carpet with absorbent powder cleaners. If the condition is severe and the color transfers to surrounding hard floors or other carpets, the problem carpet must be replaced. However, mills do an excellent job of rinsing and fixing the colors in the fabrics, and bleeding/crocking problems are quite rare.

CARPET BEETLES

Another condition that is rare but a real problem when it happens is carpet beetles. Because they only live in wool carpets, and wool use is very limited, most people never see what these beetles can do. Bare spots begin to appear very gradually everywhere—in open areas, under furniture, etc. The tufts are weak and break easily when tugged.

As the bare areas slowly enlarge, a sand-like substance the same color as the carpet appears. Small moths about ¼ inch in diameter flutter about near the carpet surface. These are the classic signs of carpet beetles, and the sand is actually beetle droppings.

The beetles live between the two backing sheets and chew at the base of the tufts, invisible from above. The carpet gradually thins out as the weakened tufts are vacuumed up. All carpets are permanently moth-proofed, but carpet beetles still show up occasionally. How they get into your house and set up shop is anyone's guess. A professional cleaner is needed to get rid of them.

CORNROWING

Cornrowing (Fig. 9-5) is a word familiar to many people who purchase a cut-pile carpet and are unhappy with the way the texture has changed. When tufts lay down in rows or cracks ½ to 2 inches apart, the change in texture is called cornrowing. It always runs across the traffic flow, but it even happens in unused rooms that are only vacuumed. It happens more with longer naps, especially those with extra-soft and fine denier yarns.

No one knows exactly what causes cornrowing, but it is generally agreed that because the cut yarn ends can lay in any direction, it is also normal for cut-pile fabrics to lay on their sides in rows. Furthermore, no one has discovered a way to remove this condition and prevent its return. A few mills will replace carpets which have

Fig. 9-5. Carpet pile that exhibits cornrowing.

cornrowed, but most will not because the replacement will most likely cornrow, too. And why should a mill replace a carpet that is not defective? The mill did not misweave it, nor did it do anything else that caused the cornrowing.

Some people get extremely upset when their carpet cornrows, others barely notice. It's just one of the things you must expect from a cut-pile carpet. But remember, not all cut-piles do it and it is impossible to tell which ones will or won't cornrow. Two neighbors can install the same carpet from different rolls and one home might experience cornrowing while the other might not.

SNAGS/SPROUTS

Snags and sprouts describe tufts that have worked up higher than the surrounding face yarns. Snags are face yarns that have been pulled from the backing by something in the home. Vacuum cleaners with sharp corners, pets, protruding nails from shoe heels, chair legs, and children can all pull out tufts and cause snags. Snags usually occur with loop-pile carpet where the foreign object pulls the loop from the backing. Snags should be clipped flush with the nap.

Sprouts are normally found with cut-pile carpets and are normal for new fabrics where loose tufts work their way out of the face pile. These should be clipped like snags. If the sprout has small blobs of latex (glue) anywhere along its length, it means that the sprout is not just an extra tuft, but that it has either been forcefully pulled from the backing, or it has worked itself loose because of a weak tuft bind.

Tuft bind is measured as the number of pounds of pull it takes to yank individual tufts from the carpet. Minimum bind for most carpets is 2 pounds, with some having minimums above 6 pounds. Two pounds might not sound like much, but it is more than enough for normal home use.

WEAK TUFT BIND

Weak tuft bind results from improper application of the latex. Sometimes the roller that applies the glue to the primary back of the carpet puts on too thin a coat, or skips and doesn't put on any at all. These weak areas eventually work loose and make holes in the face of the carpet. Sometimes the latex formula is wrong and the glue does not dry or dries out completely and turns to powder. Getting a carpet too wet by improper cleaning or flooding also breaks down the latex bond.

Checking an unused piece of scrap is the best way to tell if the problem is with the manufacturing or due to in-home problems. If the scrap is bad, it's probably a manufacturing defect. Without scrap to test, it's a guessing game because many people aren't the original owners of their carpet and don't know its history.

LINE FLAWS

All kinds of lines appear in carpets. Some are visible as soon as the carpet is rolled out; some don't show up for several days or weeks. Some go lengthwise, others widthwise; some can be serviced, some can't.

Lengthwise high lines in tufted cut-pile carpets result from nicked shearing blades during the final finishing process. Tufting needles set too low will insert longer than normal rows of yarns, too. High lines sometimes escape the watchful eyes in the mill's inspection room, only to pop up as soon as the carpet is vacuumed the first time. Some high lines run through the entire roll, and there might be multiple lines running through one roll. They are normally sheared once the carpet is installed because many lines are often cut out during the installation.

Low lines or low rows are caused by needles set too high. Because the needles insert the yarn upside down, needles set too high make rows of yarn which are shorter than the rest of the pile. Low lines appear as grooves in both cut-pile and loop fabrics. Low lines that are only a few inches long are usually retufted. If the condition is extensive, a replacement is usually necessary.

Shear Marks

The most common widthwise line besides a crease is the shear mark. The shearing blades on a tufting machine are like the blades of a reel lawn mower, which extend over the 12-foot width of the roll and shear the tips of cut-pile carpet to give the final finish. The blades can jump when the machine stops or starts, causing the stop mark.

If the carpet is gouged, it is a low shear mark and only a replacement can correct it. If part of the pile is skipped, a high shear mark is formed. Sometimes the installer cannot work around it and must hand-shear the mark. Shear marks are usually ¼ to 2 inches wide.

Some lines don't show up right away. These lines are caused by oil from various sources of the production line and aren't apparent until the oil (which is clear) attracts dirt and the line or lines get dark. This can take from 1 to 3 weeks.

The lines run lengthwise or widthwise, depending on what caused the oil to get on the carpet. They are easily removed with a dry-cleaning solvent. As one might expect, this condition is more noticeable on light carpets rather than dark colors.

FADING

Fading occurs with any color carpet and is caused by several factors. Bright sunlight is the main reason carpets fade. Sun fading makes the fabric turn green or gray, depending on the original color. Heavy draperies or sun screens on windows offer the best protection against sun fading, but since carpet is a fabric, it will eventually fade.

Most mills test their carpets to withstand a certain amount of sunlight, but none offer a guarantee against fading (unless the fabric is meant for outdoor use). High humidity or ozone concentrations also cause fading, called gas fading. Fading is most noticeable with light carpets, and is very gradual. It does not become obvious until a piece of furniture is moved. Then the area under the furniture looks green compared to the rest of the room. There is no cure for fading, other than redyeing the carpet, and redyeing is not yet perfected. Soil will make the carpet look faded in traffic areas, turning it gray. The dull areas are restored after thorough cleaning.

BUCKLING

Buckling can develop after a period of time (Fig. 9-6). Puckers around doorways and wrinkles in open areas are sure signs of buckling. It is caused by several factors. High humidity can cause even synthetic materials to relax and stretch. If the humidity is

Fig. 9-6. A loose carpet develops buckles and wrinkles.

119

temporary (like after carpet cleaning), the carpet should return to its normal tightness.

Often a soft pad allows the carpet to flex too much and eventually the carpet stretches out of shape. Or a pad can collapse underfoot and cause overflexing. Of course, if the carpet was not installed tightly enough the first time, it will quickly loosen. Restretching should correct these problems.

A carpet can also buckle if it delaminates. This means the secondary back comes away from the primary backing and air gets between the two layers. Sometimes this happens along a seam and is easy to see because you can stick your finger between the two backings. When it happens in the center of a room, the carpet will bunch up when vacuumed and will lift up easily when pulled.

Delamination occurs from ageing, from getting the carpet too wet during cleaning, or from dragging wheeled furniture constantly across the carpet (as in offices using castored chairs directly on unprotected carpet). It also happens with new carpet that has not had the secondary backing properly adhered. Most new carpet is guaranteed for 1 year against this happening.

FURNITURE MARKS

Furniture marks or dents in the carpet are evident when furniture is shifted to another location. They are easy to remove. Gently brush the crushed tufts upward. Hold a steam iron several inches from the pile allowing the steam to penetrate the yarns. Use a pocket comb to pull up the nap and restore the pile. Do not let the iron touch the pile or it may melt!

STATIC

Static is an annoying problem in most areas of the country. It is caused by two objects rubbing together, which creates an electrical charge. This happens when shoes rub against carpet. Touch a light switch or metal object, and watch the sparks fly. Static causes all types of problems for computers, too.

There are two ways to combat static. One is to increase the humidity in the affected areas. Humidifiers or even pans of water set on radiators will dramatically reduce static buildup. (Air that is too dry for carpets is not healthy for people, either.) Or anti-static sprays can be applied to the carpet. These applications typically last up to 6 months, or through one heating season. But beware. Some anti-static sprays are oil-based and can cause the carpet to soil prematurely.

Some of the new-generation nylon yarns have a permanent static protection built in. But they do not work when the humidity is very low. In fact, they are tested at the mill in a 70 percent relative humidity atmosphere. This means that if you live in a part of the country where the humidity gets below 40 to 50 percent, you will probably still need a humidifier.

ODORS

Many types of odors can plague a carpet. Even new carpets have a characteristic smell to them. Most of the time the odor disappears in a few days, but sometimes it lingers for weeks. Most mills consider this odor normal. If a person finds it too objectionable, the mill will have the carpet sprayed with a deodorant to cover up the smell until it has a chance to dissipate.

Sometimes the latex which binds the primary and secondary backings is not properly heat cured. Then the carpet gives off a "rotten egg" smell which is highly objectionable. There is no way to treat this problem, and the carpet must be replaced. Fortunately, this rarely occurs.

Pet odors are a continuing headache for some people. If the cat or dog has a favorite spot on the carpet where it likes to do its duty, the battle is constant. The odor is worse when the humidity is high because the moisture activates the organisms that live in the carpet and give off the smell. They become dormant when conditions are dry.

While vinegar and water work on small areas that are not repeatedly soaked, a professional will have to apply chemicals that actually kill the organisms, as opposed to simply masking them with a deodorant. It may be necessary to inject the chemicals between the carpet and pad to reach the soaked carpet backing. If the urine has soaked through the pad and into the floor, replacing the carpet and pad and stripping and sealing the floor, along with getting rid of the offending pet, is the only way to correct the situation.

Carpets can mildew or mold when wet, especially when jute-backed carpets are exposed to constant moisture. (Jute is a vegetable fiber and rots when soaked. It is also an excellent medium for growing mold and mildew.) That is why damp, carpeted basements smell musty. If a bathroom is carpeted, it is not unusual for the area around a tub or shower stall to turn black from mildew because of water slopping out and repeatedly wetting the carpet. If a basement floods, it is necessary to pull up the carpet as quickly as possible and dry it using special fans that blow air under the carpet. This prevents mildew as well as keeping shrinkage to a minimum.

SIDE MATCH

Side match is a condition that describes a color difference along a seam between two pieces of carpet from the same roll. It is caused by two factors. The most common concerns roll crushing along the seam. Just as roll crush can develop across the width of a carpet and make streaks, it can also occur along one side of the 12-foot width and cause a color variation across the width, making one side lighter than the other.

When the roll is cut and a piece from the darker side is seamed to the lighter side, there will be an obvious color difference along that seam. It will appear that the nap of the two pieces are running in opposite directions when, in fact, the carpeting is correctly installed. One drop will appear lighter than the other, and when viewed from the opposite direction, the color of the two pieces will reverse—what appeared light from one direction now appears dark.

This condition can be corrected by hand steaming with a Jiffy Steamer and brushing the nap to correct the lay of the pile, the same way that roll crush marks are removed. Crushing and color differences along a seam are fairly common with cut-pile carpets.

A carpet that is unevenly dyed across its width also creates a side match problem. If a carpet gets darker gradually across its width because of uneven dye, when a piece from the roll is cut and the darker side is seamed to the lighter side, the color difference will be very noticeable. The darker side will look darker from any direction. It will not reverse color the way crushed drops do. It is not possible to do anything about this problem except replace the carpet. Piece-dyed carpets are the most susceptible to uneven dye.

CHEMICALLY-INDUCED COLOR CHANGE

Spots and their removal were mentioned in Chapter 8. Stains or chemical-caused changes in the carpet are another problem and are much more difficult to handle. Everyone knows that if you spill undiluted bleach on the carpet, the color will lighten and fade. But there are many other common agents in the house which cause the carpet to change color. They include disinfectants, fade creams,

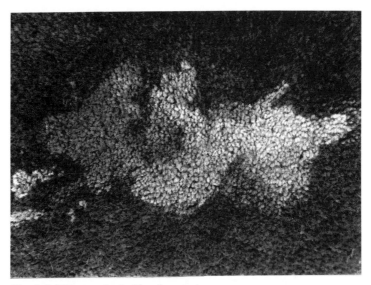
Fig. 9-7. Many products bleach carpet.

pesticides, tile cleaners, plant food, perfumes, and acne medicine (Fig. 9-7).

Some of these substances ruin the carpet right away. Others, like fade cream and acne medicine, act slowly on the fabric, lightening the carpet over a long period of time. Worse, some of the worst offenders aren't thought of as bleaching agents and little care is taken to remove them. Try to keep all foreign agents away from the carpet.

ATMOSPHERIC SOILING

Have you ever noticed soiling along a wall or steps where no one ever walks? This condition is more noticeable with light colored carpets, and is called *atmospheric soiling.* Air circulating through the house takes the path with least resistance. That can mean going between the wall and floor in a room, or along the edge of a staircase.

As the air circulates through the carpet into the crack in the floor, dust and particles of dirt begin to collect in the carpet pile along the wall. Because it acts like an air filter, the carpet gradually gets more dirty. The problem is with the design of the house, therefore, little can be done except to keep the furnace filters clean and perhaps caulk along the offending areas. But the air has to circulate, and the dirt has to go somewhere. This condition is also found under drape hems that stay in one position a long time, and along the base of furniture that sits right on top of the carpet pile.

No carpet made by machine is perfect. If examined closely enough, they all have slight imperfections. Manufacturers go to great lengths to make you a carpet that is as perfect as possible and will make you happy to put it in your home. The problems described here are quite rare. Do not think that they are found in every roll of carpet. The chances of any of these characteristics or defects showing up in your carpet should not discourage you from buying the one that you like.

Appendix A

More Money-saving Tips

I didn't get what I paid for! This very common complaint covers a wide range of problems. People think that because they paid what they consider is a lot of money for a particular carpet, there should be a certain built-in value or quality. They also think a carpet, no matter what the grade, should hold up and keep its appearance and retain its new look for several years. Also, when people buy a new home, they expect that the base grade of carpet supplied by the builder should perform well and keep its appearance for a certain length of time, usually a year or more.

The retail price of anything is determined by several factors, beginning with what the merchant pays for the item. This is the wholesale cost. The wholesale price is then marked up enough to cover business expenses such as rent, insurance, utilities, telephones, business vehicles, payroll, warehousing, and advertising—just the way a paycheck has to cover household expenses. And just as a household hopes to keep part of the paycheck for savings, a business hopes to make a profit at the end of the year.

Different retailers figure their markups differently. For example, clothing usually is marked up 2 to 2½ times, and high-fashion items often are tripled. Jewelry is commonly marked up 3 times from cost. And carpet? The carpet business is very competitive so broadloom carpet is normally marked up 1½ to 2 times from wholesale to retail.

If a carpet costs the dealer $5, the normal retail price is $8 to $10. While this might seem like gouging, remember that a lot of expenses go into running even a small carpet outlet. Many dealers get into trouble by trying to keep their prices so low that they cannot make a profit and are forced out of business. It takes a sizeable cash flow to keep the doors open every day. So carpet dealers, like all business people, look for ways to economize.

Dealer's cost normally depends upon whether the carpet is bought from the carpet manufacturer (mill) or from a distributor. Carpet mills usually have three prices for the same carpet. That's why you hardly ever see a "manufacturer's suggested retail price" on a carpet sample. The highest cost to the dealer applies only if cuts are bought.

Cuts are pieces cut off the roll at the mill and shipped for one order or one installation. Cuts cost 10 to 15 percent higher than buying a full roll. The advantage is that the cut is sold and used up on one job and there is no leftover inventory or stock to warehouse and resell. But unless the mill has a nearby warehouse, ordered cuts can take up to 3 weeks to receive.

Buying a full roll of carpet is the next best way to save on the price. Besides saving because the roll price is lower, shipping and handling costs are also lower. But this must be balanced by higher warehousing and storage costs.

Having carpet in stock also helps the retailer because the carpet can be purchased by the consumer and installed right away. This helps maintain customer satisfaction as well as cash flow. It makes sense to stock rolls of the most popular colors and order cuts for the others. That way store costs and inventories are kept down.

Buying multiple rolls of the same or various colors from a mill reduces the price even more, sometimes by an extra 5 to 10 percent, and gains the retailer another advantage—advertising money. Frequently a mill calculates the discount and matches it with a like amount to go into a kitty for advertising. The mill usually insists that its name appear in the ad. The advertising dollars build up quickly and the retailer has a successful promotion. That way the mill and retailer sell more product.

Many carpet retailers prefer to buy from a carpet distributor. Distributors carry huge inventories, either from one mill or a variety, of all qualities and colors. They are based in larger cities and sell to surrounding areas. A dealer buying from a distributor uses the distributor's stock as his own and does not need a warehouse. He can buy a cut for a small job or a roll for a large job and delivery is always immediate.

Of course, this excellent service and inventory is not free. A distributor normally buys at the mill's best price and takes a 25 to 35 percent markup to cover his expenses. Actually, that markup is very small when compared to markups taken at other levels along the distribution network, but it does add to the retailer's cost and, ultimately, to the consumer's. But there is no free lunch. "User fees" are necessary to cover the costs of doing business.

Now you understand typical costs and markups. So how do you know if the carpet you've been eyeing is worth the price tag? First, shop around and compare prices. Carpet is a "big ticket" item just like a refrigerator. Would you buy the first refrigerator you saw? Of course not. Visit or call several carpet shops. Once you know the brand and pattern it is easy to compare prices. (Of course, many stores put private labels on their carpets to discourage comparative shoppers.) If you find other stores are charging around the same price for your selection, the markup is probably fair.

If you are not in a hurry to buy because of self-imposed deadlines, you might wait to see if the carpet you want goes on sale. Most retailers have several big promotions each year—some each month! And while the sale merchandise varies from promotion to promotion, most retailers have lines that they regularly mark down.

You can always be brazen and ask the salesperson if the item you like will go on sale. Most salespeople are on commission and would rather see you return for the sales price than not return at all, so they will usually tell you what you want to know. However, some merchandise never goes on sale, for a variety of reasons. So if you are told your favorite pattern is not marked down, it could be the truth. Then it becomes a matter of deciding if the carpet is worth the price to you.

Here is another consideration regarding price and quality of carpets. New home builders offer carpeting as part of their decorating package. They all have a base grade with two or more upgrades. But what does this mean? Base and upgrade are very relative terms. One builder's top upgrade could be another's base grade. Homes that are financed through the FHA (Federal Housing Authority) must have a base grade that is approved by the FHA. The standards are minimal and vary according to carpet construction and texture, but at least it gives the consumer some basis for comparison.

A frequent complaint of consumers living in tract homes is that their upgrade carpet isn't holding up as well as their neighbor's base-grade carpet. Why? It's hard to explain because there are so many variables, but sometimes a base-grade carpet, while lighter in weight or with fewer colors has a cut-pile with a better heat-set than an upgrade one. It's confusing, but true. Just because you pay more you don't necessarily get more. And it's not the builder's fault, either. Builders buy their carpet from a mill distributor or carpet shop just like you and me, and many times know little about the carpet. Understanding what a carpet will do under normal conditions, as explained in Chapter 9 of this book, is your best defense.

As you might have guessed by now, it is difficult to put a price tag on a carpet and tell its quality. However, price ranges are easier to figure out. Level-loop carpets in the $3 to $5 per square yard range are definitely in the lower end. Medium-priced carpets sell for around $6 to $10, and anything above $10 should give you excellent service.

Cut-and-loop or cut-pile carpets usually start around $7 and go to $10 for the lower price range. Medium range for such carpets are from $10 to $15. The best carpets normally cost above $15 per square yard and the price goes as high as you want to pay, into the $50 to $100 range.

Appendix B

Effective Complaining

What should you do if you are unhappy after the carpet is installed? What is the most effective way to get the dealer to listen to your problems? What is a reasonable length of time to allow someone to handle your complaint? And what should you expect when it comes to settling a complaint?

Begin any complaint with your salesperson and work your way up the chain of command. Notify the dealer immediately if you are unhappy, or as soon as you notice the problem. (Some problems are not immediately evident.) Your salesperson wants you to be happy! Otherwise there won't be any referrals or repeat business from you.

Have the decorator, dealer, or professional carpet inspector come to your home as soon as possible to check the complaint. Some dealers handle complaints faster than others. Often the customer's attitude has a lot to do with the way a complaint is handled. Be as pleasant as possible when complaining, but be firm. The inspector checks the job to see if a problem exists with the carpet, the installation, or maintenance.

An installation complaint, such as an obvious seam, demands that the installer return to correct the problem. You can ask for a different installer if you feel the original one was incompetent or obnoxious. But the dealer usually tries to send back the same installer because it is the original installer's responsibility to correctly install the carpet before he is paid. Besides, the dealer must pay a second installer to correct the mistakes of the first one and will do everything possible to avoid any extra expense.

While it may seem odd for an installer to be able to correct what he couldn't do right the first time, most installers are good mechanics and can correct their own mistakes. There are rare occasions when an installation is done so badly that the only way to correct it is to take up the entire job and rework it.

Another possibility is that the complaint involves a misunderstanding on the part of the consumer. Improper spot cleaning, maintenance, or unrealistic expectations regarding the carpet's performance are possibilities. (Hopefully this won't happen because you have read and understood this book.) The salesperson will try to explain the situation and rectify the misunderstanding to your satisfaction.

If your complaint is with the carpet itself, things could get more involved. The problem could be what you perceive to be a physical defect, or it could relate to the carpet's performance. Call the dealer and insist that someone look at the carpet. Be patient. Expect to wait at least a week before a visit. If the salesperson cannot explain the condition the distributor or mill representative might receive a call. Each carpet mill has its own policy regarding complaints. What follows is only a typical example. No one can guarantee the mill that made your carpet handles your complaint in the manner described next.

Keep in mind that most mill reps have large sales territories to cover and therefore travel a lot. Large territories also mean that your complaint is not the only one the rep receives. A work load like this means that it could be 2 to 6 weeks before the mill rep calls to make an appointment and another couple of weeks before he actually visits your home to see the condition.

Let's assume your complaint involves a physical defect and the mill representative is knowledgeable enough to recognize it as correctable. He insists on sending out a serviceman to restore the carpet to first-quality standards. Mills reserve the right to correct a problem before they replace a carpet. (If your new car has a scratched door, the dealer repaints the scratch rather than replacing the car or the door.) This is a lot easier than pulling up the entire job and putting you through a reinstallation. Even if you don't believe the service will correct the condition, be cooperative and allow the mill the right to try. You'll be amazed at what an expert serviceman does to correct problems.

If your complaint involves a physical defect that cannot be corrected with service, the mill rep usually offers an adjustment. It is normally based on the perceived severity of the problem. Most mills initially offer an adjustment of 10 to 20 percent. You can insist on a larger adjustment if you feel the initial offer is totally unreasonable. You might get a counter offer of 30 to 40 percent. The maximum any mill ever offers is a 50 percent adjustment. Remember that if you accept an adjustment, the matter is ended as far as the mill is concerned. The defect remains in the carpet after the adjustment money is spent.

If you feel an adjustment will not make you happy, you can insist on a replacement. The mill then requests a carpet inspection from an independent carpet inspection company to make sure your complaint is valid. Qualified inspectors have been trained not only to recognize carpet and installation problems, but to service and correct these problems whenever possible. The inspector is unbiased because he does not work for the mill, the dealer, or the installer.

After the inspector examines your carpet, he writes a report, containing his evaluation of the problem and his suggestion of what is needed to close the complaint, including replacement. Most mills follow the inspector's recommendations. If the inspector recommends a replacement, you get one. If the inspector feels the complaint is not valid, the mill politely tells you it can do no more for you.

If you qualify for a replacement, you receive an exact duplicate of what you purchased, including quality and color. Most mills do not allow the consumer to switch to a different carpet. Also, carpet mills only replace material, not labor. It is up to your carpet dealer to supply the labor for any reinstallation, and he receives no reimbursement for any lost labor. Some dealers replace the carpet with no additional labor charges to you. Some ask that you pay for the labor to reinstall the replacement carpet, or at least split the cost with them. (Since the pad and tackstrip remain, the cost should be less than the original installation price.) This point is something you should ask the dealer about when you initially purchase the carpet. Then you won't have any surprises if a replacement is necessary later.

What can you do when the mill denies your claim? The dealer could simply go along with the mill's decision and say that nothing more can be done. But if the dealer values you as a customer and thinks you do have a valid claim, the dealer could replace the carpet on his own and negotiate with the mill later. The dealer is taking a great risk because, besides the labor costs for the replacement, the dealer could end up with a pile of used carpet in his warehouse that the mill refuses to accept. But at least the dealer has a happy, satisfied customer who will tell friends about the wonderful service and will come back again for another carpet purchase.

When you have a carpet complaint, remember to be reasonable, cooperative, and patient. You are dealing with other human beings and, to use an old adage, you can catch more flies with sugar than with vinegar.

Appendix C

Repairing a Burn

What should you do about a stain or burn in the carpet? Should you just ignore the problem, or is there a way to fix the area? What if a log pops from the fireplace and burning coals are scattered across the room which leave many small burns?

Fortunately, there is a way to invisibly repair most burns and stains up to 4 inches in diameter. (Larger problems still need to be repaired by an installer.) The following is a step-by-step method that is simple, though tedious, and is unknown to most installers and repairmen. Homeowners who don't know anything about tufted carpet can, with a little practice and some scrap carpet, repair their own carpet without pulling it up from the floor. If you don't want to do it yourself, at least you will know what to expect from the person you have hired to do the job. (You'd better ask the serviceman to make sure he knows how!)

Let's assume you've had a party and a guest has left behind a memento—a burn in the center of the family room carpet (Fig. C-1). At first you are angry and horrified. Then you remember that some scrap pieces remain from the installation, and you decide to fix the burn. After all, who wants a burn in carpet which is practically brand new?

First, you will need some tools and supplies: an awl or ice pick, a pair of small, sharp scissors, a carpet knife (preferably with a changeable, razor-type blade), and a hot-melt glue gun or liquid latex rubber or a fairly thick contact cement (waterproof) (Fig. C-2).

Fig. C-1. A cigarette burn in carpet.

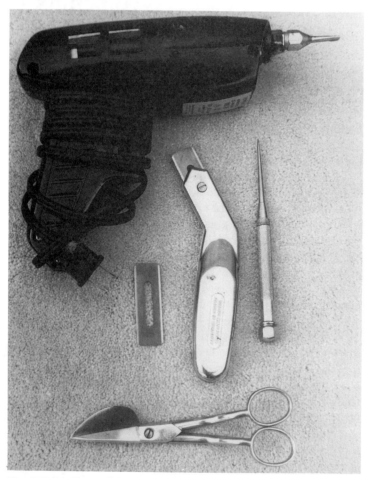

Fig. C-2. Tools needed to repair tufted carpet.

Step 1. Using the awl, separate the rows of yarn around the burn (Fig. C-3). They should form a square or rectangle because most of the time the rows run in a straight line.

Step 2. Take the carpet knife and cut through the primary backing between the rows of yarn, being careful to leave all the tufts on both sides of your cut. With a sharp blade and a little practice, it is easy to "feel" the blade cutting only through the primary backing. *Do not cut through the secondary backing!*

Step 3. Cut between the rows all the way around the burn.

Step 4. Gently pull the tufts on the burn-side of the cut. This way you gently separate the yarn and the primary backing from the secondary back and you can see if any areas need more cutting (Fig. C-4). It may be necessary to use the scissors to cut through tufts which are buried below the primary backing and were not cut when the knife went through the primary backing.

Step 5. Once you have cut all around the burn and made sure the primary and face yarns are cut from the secondary back, you can lift the entire area—primary and face yarns—away from the secondary backing, that will be exposed (Fig. C-5). You may need to scrape some latex away from the secondary backing with the awl to make the area completely clean.

Step 6. Now peel off the secondary backing from a corner of the scrap and look for the parallel, lengthwise rows of yarn which are tufted into the primary backing (Fig. C-6). (Sometimes the tufts stick to the secondary backing and pull through the primary leaving

Fig. C-3. Separate the rows of yarn to expose the primary backing.

135

Fig. C-4. Cut only through the primary backing and lift the face yarn and primary backing away from the secondary backing.

Fig. C-5. Completely remove the affected area.

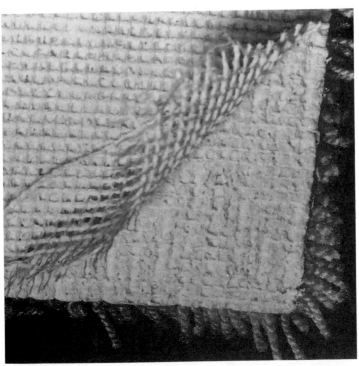

Fig. C-6. Peel the secondary backing off the scrap carpet that replaces the burned area.

holes, so be gentle and pull the secondary backing off slowly.) A thick coating of latex might make the rows hard to see. The rows run down the length of the fabric and help determine the lay of the nap. For small repairs up to 1 inch, it is not important to put the new piece in with the nap running in the right direction. But larger repairs come out better if the nap runs correctly. Once you have found length and width, it is easy to brush the pile lengthwise and see when the pile lays "up" and "down." (The flat nap of loop-pile carpet makes it very hard to find pile direction.) If the carpet has a sculptured or printed pattern you must, of course, match the pattern with the scrap piece.

Step 7. Take the scissors and cut pile-side up between the rows of yarn to make a patch a little larger than what you removed from the installed carpet. Put the patch against the cut area and measure, then trim the patch to the correct size. When the piece is the right size, you can slip the patch into place and it is invisible. Remove the patch.

Fig. C-7. Fit the new piece into the cut out area.

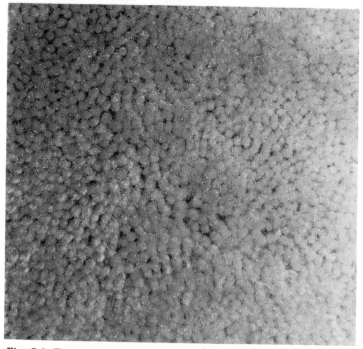

Fig. C-8. The replacement is completely invisible.

138

Step 8. Now carefully apply your hot-melt glue or latex to the exposed secondary backing. Use Q-Tips to apply latex or contact cement. Do not get any on the surrounding face pile. Make sure the glue covers all corners and edges completely, and brush the face yarns away from the glue so they do not get stuck in the glue when you set in the new piece. When you set in the new piece (Fig. C-7), the *glue should completely meet all cut edges* and bind the face yarns tightly. With cut-piles, any missed tufts could fall out, making a hole. Loop piles can also snag and pull out.

Step 9. Use the awl to press the edges of the new piece firmly into the glue and make certain that everything has adhered to the secondary backing. Gently press the center of the patch so that no bubbles remain under it. When finished, the pile height of the new piece should match the surrounding pile exactly (Fig. C-8). Little or no trimming should be necessary because the secondary backing keeps the patch at the correct level. (That is why you removed the secondary back from your scrap.)

Once the glue is dry, the new piece is as strong as the original. You can vacuum and clean it without worry. The new area is invisible because all the face yarns are in place and the seams are completely covered by the pile.

Note: Whenever you get new carpet, its a good idea to expose a piece of scrap to air and sunlight and clean it with your installed carpet. This way both pieces pack evenly and the scrap will match the installed carpet more closely when you use it for a repair.

Glossary

acrylic—Fiber produced from acrylonitrile, which is made from air, coal, oil, water, and limestone. The Federal Trade Commission defines acrylic as a manufactured fiber in which the fiber-forming substance is any long chain synthetic polymer composed of at least 85 percent acrylonitrile units by weight. Other chemicals are added to improve dyeability. Some acrylic fibers are dry spun and some are wet spun. Most are used in staple form and are crimped before cutting into staple. Brand names include Acrilan (Monsanto), Creslan (American Cyanamid), Orlon (Du Pont), and Zefran (Dow Badiche).

Axminster—A method of weaving using unlimited colors. The tufts are woven to the back in a way which imitates hand knotting.

backing—Kraftcord, cotton, jute, or synthetic materials used to form the back of the carpet. The weave of the Wilton loom forms the backing. Tufted carpet has two backings, the primary and secondary.

back seams—Made when the carpet is turned over face down. They are generally less visible than face seams.

BCF—Bulked continuous filament yarns. Any continuous filament yarn which has been crimped, bulked, curled, or otherwise been treated in order to make the yarn feel bulkier.

beck—A container holding dye into which an entire roll of carpet (unbacked) is placed.

berber—Woven or tufted looped carpet made from nubby plied yarns.

binding—A strip of cloth sewed over a raw edge to keep it from ravelling. Binding is used when cutting carpet up to make into area rugs.

birdcage—The end of a stair rail where the banister curves into a spiral.

broadloom—Carpet made wider than 54 inches. It used to indicate high quality, but that designation is out of date. Twelve-foot width is the most common today, with fifteen-foot widths available occasionally. The wide widths allow fewer seams in large rooms.

buckles—Ridges or wrinkles that appear in a carpet after it is installed wall-to-wall. The condition is caused by either faulty material or improper installation.

bulking—Crimping or curling yarns to produce additional fullness.

bullnose—A bottom step formed by extending the nosing well over the riser. It is usually curved at the end and is wider than the rest of the steps.

burling—Hand tufting face yarns into any void areas, either at the mill or after installation.

carpet—A general term for fabrics used to cover flooring.

cellulosic fibers—Rayon, acetate, and triacetate, all derived from wood. These fibers are not good for carpet yarns. Instead, noncellulosic fibers made from chemicals are used for carpet yarns.

chain binders—Yarns running lengthwise (warpwise) in the back of the carpet. They bind all construction yarns together. The chain binders alternate over and under the weft (widthwise binding) and filling yarns, pulling the pile yarns down and the stuffer yarns up for a tight weave.

construction—The process used to combine face yarns and backing fibers into a carpet. Refers to both woven and tufted carpet.

continuous filament—Synthetic yarn drawn from liquid into a continuous length. It does not shed when spun into carpet yarn. Silk is the only natural continuous filament fiber.

cornrowing—An effect produced when the carpet pile lays down in rows or grooves perpendicular to the traffic flow. The corrugated look can occur in any cut-pile fabric. It is not a defect, although most people agree it is unsightly. The exact cause is unknown and there is no permanent method to correct it.

crab—A hand tool used in areas too small for a knee kicker.

crimp—A method used to create a bulkier yarn. This helps cover more carpet with less yarn and helps spun staple yarns to better interlock.

crocking—Improperly dyed carpet in which the dye runs. Dry crocking occurs under dry conditions, often rubbing off on socks or clothes. Wet crocking is noticeable only when the fabric is wet.

cross-seams—Seams made at the widthwise ends of carpet.

delustering—Reducing the brightness of synthetic fibers through chemical means. This gives a more wool-like appearance.

denier—The weight of 9000 meters of yarn expressed in grams. The higher the denier, the larger the diameter of the yarn. The ''soft hand'' carpets use a low denier yarn.

drop match—A pattern that repeats diagonally across the width of the carpet, with each pattern figure dropping a certain distance before repeating again. All patterned carpet must be matched at the seams.

dry cleaning—A method of cleaning carpet by applying a dry substance impregnated with cleaning solvents to the face pile. The dry compound absorbs soil and is vacuumed up. Works best for touching up between thorough cleanings.

Du Pont 501—Brand name for Du Pont's first continuous filament yarn developed in 1958. In 1965 it became the certification mark for carpets that meet or exceed performance standards of Du Pont.

dye—Coloring or pigment used to color fibers, yarns, or carpets. Includes natural and synthetic pigments.

dyeing—Process of applying color to carpet face yarns. The most common methods include:

1). *cationic:* A chemical that is added to yarn, allowing it to react to dyes differently than untreated yarn. When mixed together, the two yarns make two colors from one batch of dye.

2). *continuous:* Applying all the dye in one continuous process.

3). *piece:* Carpet is dyed after tufting or weaving, in one piece. This is done in a dye beck, or by using the continuous dyeing method.

4). *resist:* Treating carpet pile to resist and repel dye from specific areas to form a pattern.

5). *solution:* Adding color to liquid synthetics before drawing into fibers, producing extremely colorfast yarns.

6). *space:* Dyeing long strands of continuous filament yarns several colors before tufting or weaving to create a tweed effect.

7). *stock:* Coloring large vats of staple fiber before it is spun into yarn.

8). *TAK:* After basic dyeing, a German-developed method adds other colors by controlled dripping.

9). *vat:* This is a type of dye, not a manufacturing process. Vat dyes are used for stock, skein, and solution dyeing, and are extremely fast dyestuffs.

10). *yarn or skein:* This is the oldest type of dye method used in carpet manufacture. Skeins of yarn are dyed before they are tufted or woven into carpet.

embossed—A pattern formed when heavy twisted tufts (frieze) are used against a background of straight yarns to create an engraved appearance.

face seams—Seams made from the face instead of the back of the carpet. They generally are more visible than back seams.

fading—Loss of color due to strong light, chemicals, or gases.

fiber—natural or synthetic strands of material used in making textiles, such as carpet.

filament—A single continuous strand of fiber, natural (silk) or man-made.

filament yarn—Two or more continuous filaments twisted together.

filling yarn—Weft (widthwise) yarns used with the chain (warp) yarns to bind the face yarns to the backing yarns of woven carpets.

fill piece—A strip of carpet side-seamed to broadloom and used when the area to be carpeted is wider than the standard width of carpet.

flocked—A low-pile carpet made by adhering one end of face yarns to a fabric using glue.

fluff—Lint or fuzz characteristic of new carpets. It is loose ends of face pile left after manufacture. Frequent vacuuming greatly reduces or stops the shedding.

frieze—Refers to both the short, tightly twisted yarns and the texture of carpet produced using the rough, nubby yarns.

fuzzed—The matted, stringy look after carpet yarns split or untwist.

gauge—In tufted carpet, it is the distance between the rows of pile yarn and is measured in fractions of an inch. A ⅛ gauge fabric has eight rows per one inch section of width; a ⅒ gauge carpet has 10 rows per inch. It is the equivalent of pitch in woven goods.

greige goods—Undyed tufted carpet without a secondary back.

grin—A condition where the rows of face yarns separate to expose the carpet backing. Most common when carpet is installed over sharp edges, such as stairs.

hand—The way a carpet feels when handled. Thickness, pile height, yarn texture, and backing stiffness all affect the hand.

heat-set—Applying pressure, heat and/or steam to plied yarns in order to set the twist. This keeps the yarns of cut-pile carpets from fraying and untwisting and helps maintain the original appearance longer.

high-density foam—Foam pad with a minimum weight of 38 ounces per square yard and a minimum density of 17 pounds per cubic foot.

high-low—A textured carpet with more than one pile height, usually high and low loops or high cut-pile with low loop areas (also known as cut-and-loop).

hydrophobic fibers—Those fibers, such as nylon and olefin, that do not absorb water.

indoor-outdoor carpet—Outdoor carpet.

Jacquard—A mechanism on Wilton looms for making patterns. A cardboard roll with holes activates a selecting device that pulls the indicated face yarns to the surface, working on the same principle as the music roll in a player piano.

jute—A fiber derived from the hemp plant in India and the Far East. It is used in woven carpet for backing yarns. Jute is woven into sheets resembling burlap to form primary and secondary backings for tufted carpet.

knee-kicker—A short device with gripper teeth on one end and a cushion on the other used by installers to stretch carpet in small areas, by putting the teeth into the pile and bumping the padded end with the knee.

knitted—A carpet made by knitting the backing yarn, stitching yarn, and face yarn together to make a loop pile. This fabric is generally used in commercial installations.

latexing—The process of applying latex to a carpet backing. The latex locks in face yarns and also acts as a glue when laminating a secondary backing.

level-loop—Woven or tufted looped-pile, with all tufts the same height.

loom—A device used to make fabric by crossing warp and weft yarns at right angles to form pile yarns attached to a backing. Can be hand or power driven.

loop-pile—Woven or tufted pile of uncut loops.

lustre—The sheen or brightness of a carpet, ranging from low lustre to wool and delustered nylons, to high lustre nylons and polyesters. Duller lustres hide soil better.

matting—A condition that exists when plied yarns untwist and become crushed, entangled, and fused. It occurs because of a defective heat-set or through normal use.

mercerizing—A special finish used on wool for lustre and strength.

mill end—A piece of carpet less than a short roll but longer than a remnant, usually between 9 and 20 feet long.

modacrylic—Fibers made from hydrocarbon resins that are combinations of acrylonitrile and chemicals such as vinyl chloride or vinylidene chloride. This fiber is defined by the Federal Trade Commission as: "A manufactured fiber in which the fiber-forming substance is any long chain synthetic polymer composed of less than 85 percent but at least 35 percent by weight of acrylonitrile units." It is blended with acrylic fibers to increase fire resistance of the acrylic. Brands include Acrilan (Monsanto), Dynel (Union Carbide), and Verel (Eastman).

monofilament—A single continuous strand of fiber.

moresque—A carpet texture produced by combining single strands of differently colored yarns to form one multicolored yarn end. It creates a salt and pepper look.

multifilament—Bulked continuous filament yarns.

nap—The face yarns or pile of a carpet. The nap acquires a "lay" or direction as the carpet moves off the machine and is wound into a roll.

needle-punched—A carpet made by laying face yarns onto a backing material and using needles to punch in and lock the face yarns to the backing.

nosing—The place where the top of a stair riser meets the front of the stair tread.

nylon—A synthetic fiber made from hydrocarbon compounds from the polyamide family. The two main types are nylon-6.6 and nylon-6 carpet fiber. It is extruded from a solution into filaments. The Federal Trade Commission defines nylon as: "A manufactured fiber in which the fiber forming substance is any long chain synthetic polyamide having recurring amide groups as an integral part of the polymer chain.'' Nylon accounts for almost 90 percent of all tufted carpet made in this country. Brand names include ANSO, ANSO IV, and ANSO IV HP (Allied Corp.), Antron and Antron III (Du Pont), Zefstat (Dow Badische), Ultron (Monsanto), and Enkaloft and Enkalure II (American Enka).

olefin—There are two types of olefin fibers, polypropylene and polyethylene, made from propylene and ethylene gases. Polypropylene is the olefin fiber used for textiles. The Federal Trade Commission defines olefin as ''A manufactured fiber in which the fiber-forming substance is any long chain synthetic polymer composed of at least 85 percent by weight of ethylene, propylene, or other olefin units except amorphous (noncrystalline) polyolefins qualifying in another category.'' Brands include Herculon (Hercules), Vectra (Vectra), Marvess (Phillips), and Patlon (Amoco Fabrics Co.). Olefins account for less than 5 percent of all tufted carpet.

pad—A cushion placed under carpet to prevent abrasion and provide softness. It is made from felted cattle hair, jute, wool, rubber, or foam.

pile—The wear surface of a carpet made by the yarn ends of the face or nap.

pile crush—Compression of pile thickness due to heavy traffic. It is normal for any carpet.

pile height—The height of the face pile measured from the top of the backing to the tip of the pile.

pilling—A condition where strands of the face fiber become entangled with one another causing a rough surface similar to an old sweater. Pills should be clipped, never pulled, from the pile surface.

pitch—In woven carpet, the number of warp (lengthwise) threads per 27-inch width of carpet. A higher number indicates a closer weave.

plied yarn—Two or more single yarns twisted together. Plied yarns are normally heat-set to keep the yarns twisted under heavy traffic. The ply number tells how many single ends are twisted together: two-ply, three-ply, etc.

plush—A cut-pile fabric made from nonheat-set singles spun yarn. It has a very smooth surface and is longer than a velvet.

polyester—A synthetic fiber made from long chain hydrocarbons. It is extruded from a solution into filaments which are melt spun. The Federal Trade Commission defines polyester as: ''A manufactured fiber in which the fiber-forming substance is any long chain synthetic polymer composed of at least 85 percent by weight of an ester of a dihydric alcohol and terephthalic acid.'' Brands include Dacron by Du Pont and Trevira Star from Hoechst.

pooling—Also called watermarking, shading, or pile reversal. Normal for cut-pile fabrics, it is a dark, irregular area caused by the face pile reversing direction usually in a traffic area.

power stretcher—A tool used to stretch large areas of carpet over the pad. It consists of a head with gripper teeth, tubular extensions, and a padded end. The padded end is placed against the wall opposite from the carpet to be stretched, with the tubes extended across the room and the gripper teeth in the pile. A lever attached to the head allows the installer to stretch the carpet using very little effort. This tool should be used in all possible rooms to assure proper stretch.

primary backing—In tufted carpet, the woven or nonwoven sheet into which the face yarns are tufted. It is made from jute or polypropylene.

printed carpet—Carpet with patterns applied using various printing systems.

pucker—A wrinkle in a seam caused by one side being longer than the other.

random sheared—In looped carpet, a pattern made by shearing only some of the loops into cut-pile. The looped areas look lighter than the sheared areas.

remnant—A piece of carpet less than 9 feet long.

repeat—In patterned carpet, the frequency and distance that the pattern recurs, measured lengthwise.

resilience—The ability of carpet to return to its original texture and thickness after being crushed by traffic or furniture.

restretch—Carpet stretching after the original installation to correct wrinkles or loose fit. A power stretcher should be used whenever possible.

riser—the vertical portion of a step.

roll crush—Pile distortion, usually in the form of widthwise bands or streaks, which can be found in any type or quality of carpet, although cut-pile fabrics are more prone to roll crush. It is self correcting when the condition is slight. Only wool and nylon piles can be corrected by applying steam.

round wire—In woven carpet, the wire over which face yarns are drawn to form looped-pile.

rug—Any loose-laid carpet.

saxony—A cut-pile made with plied, heat-set yarns having good tuft tip definition. Saxonies are longer than plushes, although many people call smoother finished saxonies plushes.

sculptured—A patterned carpet made by using high and low pile areas.

secondary backing—The backing that is visible when the carpet is turned over. It is made from woven jute or olefin, or from nonwoven olefin. It is attached to the primary backing by latex and adds stiffness and dimensional stability to tufted carpet.

seconds—Also known as irregulars. Carpet which does not meet a manufacturer's first-quality standards because of off-quality defects ranging from color variation to poor backing lamination.

selvedge—The side edges of carpet that are not tufted. The selvedge is normally trimmed off at the mill.

serging—Stitching heavy yarn around the cut edge of a carpet to prevent ravelling.

shading—A color difference in the carpet pile caused by yarn ends in one area laying in a different direction than the rest of the pile. Light reflecting off the sides of the yarn produces a lighter color than light which reflects off the yarn tips to make a darker color. Shading is normal and characteristic for all cut-pile carpets. When severe, it is known as watermarking or pooling.

shampooing—The oldest method of carpet cleaning utilizing a rotary brush to apply a shampoo solution to the carpet pile. Its main drawbacks are overwetting and the residue that is left behind that causes the carpet to quickly resoil.

shearing—The process in which the carpet is drawn under revolving cutting blades similar to a reel lawn mower, producing a smooth finish.

short roll—A piece of carpet shorter than a full roll but longer than a remnant, usually twenty to forty feet.

shot—In woven carpets, the number of weft (widthwise) yarns in relation to each row of lengthwise pile tufts. A two-shot fabric has two weft yarns for each row of pile tufts. A three-shot fabric has three weft yarns for each row of tufts. More shots help make a heavier fabric.

side seams—Seams made along the lengthwise side of the carpet.

singles yarn—One-ply face yarns used in velvet and plush constructions.

skein-dyed yarn—Carpet face yarns dyed while wound in skein form by immersion in large dye vats.

soil retardant—A chemical sprayed onto the carpet surface that slows the soiling rate and offers some protection against spills and stains. It does not make the carpet stain-proof, and is removed after several cleanings.

solution dye—Synthetic fibers dyed in a liquid state before being drawn into filaments. Dye and fiber become one and the resulting yarn is extremely colorfast.

space-dyed—Yarn dyed alternately two or more colors along its length. A tweed effect results when tufted into carpet.

spinnerette—A device with a perforated head, similar to a shower, through which a liquid fiber is extruded to form filaments.

spinning—1. The process where short-length staple fibers (wool, cotton) are made into long strands of yarn. 2. In synthetic fiber production, spinning is the extrusion of a liquid substance through a spinnerette and the hardening of it into fibers. There are three forms of spinning: wet, dry, and melt. *Wet spinning* extrudes fibers into a chemical bath which hardens them. *Dry spinning* hardens the filament after extrusion by passing the fibers through solvent that has been evaporated in the air. Some acrylics are dry spun. *Melt spinning* is a process where the fiber forming substance (polymer chips) is melted, extruded, and hardened by cooling. Nylon and polyester are made this way.

sprouts—Long ends of yarn which protrude above the pile surface and which were not removed during shearing. They should be cut with scissors, never pulled. Sprouting is a defect only if excessive and unserviceable.

staple yarn—Short lengths (3 to 8 inches) of fiber that are spun into yarn using a modified worsted system.

static—An electrical charge produced by shoes rubbing against carpet pile and discharged when a person touches a conductive ground, such as a light switch or doorknob.

stay tacking—Temporarily nailing one section of a stretched carpet to hold it in place until the remainder is stretched into place. Used in large, especially commercial, installations.

steam cleaning—A method of injecting pressurized hot water mixed with a cleaning solution into the carpet pile, and removing most of the solution and soil by vacuum extraction. When done properly, this is the safest and most effective way to clean wall-to-wall carpet.

stock-dyed yarn—Yarn made from previously dyed staple yarn.

streak—A lengthwise or widthwise defect in a carpet, caused by uneven dye, defects, machinery oil, or crushed yarns.

texture—Any surface effect that gives added interest to the pile over and above that provided by the basic design or colorations, including high and low yarns, brocading, shearing, and yarn twist and dimensions.

three-quarter goods—Before broadloom, the first power looms made carpet 27 inches or three-quarters of a yard wide. Still used today, it does not indicate any level of quality.

tip-shear—A pattern created by shearing loops of a carpet so that the pile is part cut and part uncut. Shearing produces a dappled effect and can be random or in a definite pattern.

tone on tone—A pattern made by using two or more shades of the same color.

traffic patterns—The main usage areas of an installation, and the wear patterns which develop from such use.

tread—The horizontal part of a stair upon which the foot steps.

tuft bind—The force, measured in pounds, needed to pull a tuft of yarn from the carpet backing. Acceptable strength varies according to construction methods.

tufting—Face yarns which are stitched by rows of needles into a backing material (today almost exclusively twelve feet wide) and secured by a coating of latex rubber. Over 95 percent of all carpet sold in the U.S. are tufted because the tufting machines run at a much greater speed than looms, thus lowering the price.

tufts—The cut or uncut face pile of a carpet.

twist—The number of turns per inch in carpet yarn, usually four to six.

vat dye—Refers to a very colorfast type of dye rather than a dye technique. Stock dyeing, skein dyeing, and solution dyeing are all done with vat dyes.

velvet—A short pile carpet woven on a velvet loom. It is the simplest of all carpet weaves and is made in solid colors. Woven with wires, a looped pile is made when the wires are removed. A cut-pile is created when knife blades on the ends of the wires cut the loops.

virgin wool—As defined by the Wool Products Labeling Act, virgin wool or new wool has never been used or reclaimed from any spun, woven, knitted, felted, manufactured, or used product. Does not indicate any quality standard.

warp—The yarns running lengthwise in a fabric.

watermark—A severe example of shading. The affected area appears dark and seems to have had a bucket of water poured on it. This is not a defect of cut-pile carpet, although many people find the condition unsightly.

weaving—A manufacturing technique whereby lengthwise and widthwise yarns are interlaced to form a carpet. Examples are velvet, Axminster, and Wilton weaves.

weft—In woven carpet, the widthwise yarns that weave in the warp threads and lock in the pile yarns.

Wilton—A type of carpet weave made on a loom using a series of perforated cards, similar to computer punch cards that automatically select different colors (from two to six) of yarn to form the design. While one color is raised, the others run through the center and back of the carpet.

wool—The hair of sheep and the yarn made from the fibers of the fleece.

woolen systems—Yarn that is spun from short fibers, either natural or synthetic, and then interlocked and twisted as much as possible during the spinning operation.

worsted system—A method of spinning yarn from longer staple that has been carded to lay the fibers parallel. The fibers are combed to remove shorter fibers, and are spun and twisted into yarn. The fibers stand up in a cut-pile carpet and do not shed as much as short staple yarns.

yarn—A continuous strand spun from staple fibers or continuous filaments used as carpet face pile.

TS
1775.5
.R48
1988

Index

TS
1775.5
.R48
1988

Edited by Jo